Embrace the suck of the journey.

SUCCESS PSYCHE

others in the process of his presentations. I've known Jay for over 15 years and witnessed that many of his decisions are rooted in helping others. Jay never boasted about doing this or that but would ask what you think about this or that idea. When he laid out an idea, you'd think, "That is what I need/want but didn't know how to do it or even where to begin." Jay is an amazing, considerate, and thoughtful leader who cares about his people, family, and staff. He always has a hello and is the kind of man you want to be around. You want his thoughts on your questions!" **—Robert Varich**

"Over 20 years of working with Jay, I have seen firsthand how the guidance and positive perspective he has on managing and working with our team and clients has allowed us to grow into multiple office locations, regions, and then to additional businesses. His push in partnering and training with other professionals consistently allows us all to grow at our crafts. I wouldn't be where I was today without his mentoring and constant (and loving) nagging."

—Amanda Strader

"I've been blessed to have known Jay for over 15 years. What started out as friendship quickly turned into mentorship. His winning mentality is contagious. Jay is an all-or-nothing professional with a deep focus, commitment, and outstanding inspiration. I've gained numerously from his willingness to share his thoughts and ideas, never afraid to shoot you straight. Want to GROW immensely? Jay Adkins' *Success Psyche* is the ultimate book for you." **—Chris Parish**

"Working with and being mentored by Jay Adkins during the most critical years of my working years is what has catapulted me to where

I am today in business. His ruthless desire for excellence daily in every aspect made everyone around him aspire to be more, do more, and dream bigger. It also rubbed off on me like words can't explain. It helped me look at the bad from a positive angle. It taught me that success is fought for and earned every single day and that if you want it badly enough, there is nothing you can't manifest in your life. I observed the consistent habits that were non-negotiable for him and applying them in my life transformed my way of feeling, thinking, acting. This has led to a whole different outlook on what success really is. I was blessed with the opportunity to be side-by-side a legend and pick at his brain. Jay wholeheartedly opened up to me and taught me more than I could've ever asked for." **—Danny Robledo**

"I've known Jay Adkins for several years, and while we're in the same industry, he gets the kinds of things done that I and others only dream about! I've never known him to accept "no" while pursuing his success. Jay couples this drive with unusual compassion and caring for people. He makes the world a better place!" **—Stan Tebow**

"Jay Adkins is excellence personified. I have had the distinct pleasure of getting to know Jay personally and professionally over the past few years. Regardless of what he is working on or who he is working with, he has an unshakable desire to leave the world a better place than he found it. Using the old cliché of "a rising tide raises all ships," Jay is the tide, always trying to make those around him better than before. Do not mistake his intensity as intimidating, which is just how he approaches life. Showing up as the best version of himself in anything he does." **—Chris Marok**

"Jay Adkins is, simply put, one of the smartest and most successful people I've ever met. He commands that unique blend of business savvy and street smarts while at the same time being both data-driven and super intuitive. As Rudyard Kipling once stated, Jay is also that rare person that can "talk with crowds and keep his virtue or walk with kings—nor lose the common touch." He so freely opens his heart, soul, experience, and success to uplift others, making him super special. Jay embodies and lives the Success Psyche every moment of his life and learning from him. That mindset has been, quite frankly, transformative for me in every aspect of my life."

—Greg Gray

"Disciplined. Inquisitive. Relentless. These are just a few of the words that jump to mind when I think of Jay. In the 20 years that I've known him, I've witnessed the exponential growth of both his business and Jay individually as a mentor and leader. Admittedly, in the early days, I found it odd when a casual conversation between us would somehow pivot to how I was tracking towards my annual goals. At first, this threw me off, but I quickly realized that his mind is constantly analyzing and looking for best practices. He is relentless, and most importantly CONSISTENT, in his pursuit of excellence. Over the past few years, he has channeled that energy into coaching and mentoring others. Whether it's his book club or the podcast he started, I've enjoyed seeing Jay expand his reach to impact a broader spectrum of people. And if I were to name the traits that make Jay uniquely qualified to share his success tactics, they would be having a positive mindset and being consistent."

—Darren Mock

SUCCESS PSYCHE

MASSIVE ACTIONS THAT WILL ILLUMINATE YOUR PATH TO SUCCESS

JAY ADKINS

NEW YORK

LONDON • NASHVILLE • MELBOURNE • VANCOUVER

SUCCESS **PSYCHE**

Massive Actions That Will Illuminate Your Path to Success

Published in New York, New York, by Morgan James Publishing. Morgan James is a trademark of Morgan James, LLC. www.MorganJamesPublishing.com

Proudly distributed by Ingram Publisher Services.

Morgan James BOGO™

A **FREE** ebook edition is available for you or a friend with the purchase of this print book.

_____

CLEARLY SIGN YOUR NAME ABOVE

Instructions to claim your free ebook edition:
1. Visit MorganJamesBOGO.com
2. Sign your name CLEARLY in the space above
3. Complete the form and submit a photo of this entire page
4. You or your friend can download the ebook to your preferred device

ISBN 9781631957550 case laminate
ISBN 9781631957543 paperback
ISBN 9781631957567 ebook
Library of Congress Control Number:
2021945703

Cover and Interior Design by:
Marisa Jackson

Morgan James is a proud partner of Habitat for Humanity Peninsula and Greater Williamsburg. Partners in building since 2006.

Get involved today! Visit MorganJamesPublishing.com/giving-back

I DEDICATE THIS BOOK TO MY MOTHER,
DOROTHY ADKINS.

She was a wonderful mother who loved *everyone*. She would have helped every single person on the planet if she had the chance. My mom saw every person as we all should: They are all human beings who deserve to be heard. So, she helped them the best way she knew how—which was to listen to them and to be kind.

My mom left a lasting legacy in this world by constantly reminding me, "Kindness is free and easy." I feel so thankful to have had such a wise, loving mother. She was an inspiration to me and to everyone else who knew her.

Because of her selfless ways, she has inspired me to carry on her mission to help as many people as possible realize they have something inside of them that they don't know exists. I hope that my work and *Success Psyche* will help fulfill her desire to help anyone in need. I also hope this will allow people to help themselves.

THIS IS MY WHY.

These incredible souls I get to share life with are a big part of my WHY—my purpose. I'm dedicated to changing lives because of my dedication and commitment to being the best and then *better* version of myself each and every day for my family. These beautiful human beings are what get me out of bed in morning and make life absolutely phenomenal.

I want to do better because my kids and wife are watching. I'm their example. I also want them to be the CEOs of their own lives, so I have a responsibility to model the correct behavior in *my* life first. Whatever else you do today, commit to defining your why and letting it become the catalyst that shapes your legacy.

ACKNOWLEDGMENTS

I would like to thank my wife, Ximena, for supporting me on this book-writing journey. This project took time away from our family, but you stood beside me and my longstanding dream to write something that will impact lives for years to come.

I would also like to thank all the people who told me certain things were impossible. Some of you, like Chris Burke, knew this is the language that drives me. Others believed it was impossible for *them*, so they thought (or possibly wished) it would be the same for me. Those doubts became my jet fuel.

I would also like to thank my good friend Greg Gray for being my constant sounding board—for always giving me honest feedback that sharpens me.

Thanks to Chris Burke for being a excellent mentor, leader, and example of what it takes to be a great entrepreneur. You are the one who told me how important kids are and how having my own would transform my life for the better. I had no idea what you meant until it happened—and they are now, far and away, the best things in my life.

Last but not least, I'd like to acknowledge my three beautiful daughters. To my first-born Jordan—I was so young and learned so much from you. I also know I wasn't the best father 27 years ago. But because of you, I have become a better man and a better father. To Luna and Skye—everything I do is for your mother and for your legacy. I know I'm on stage, and you are watching everything I do. I know I'm your example. You have given me purpose, and you have shown me unconditional love.

Ximena, Jordan, Jett, Cristan, Luna, and Skye, you are my why.

TABLE OF CONTENTS

START HERE!

Massive Actions Become Mindful Habits xvii

ONE

Learn that Success is a Snowflake 1

TWO

Outline Your Terms of Success 31

THREE

Realize You Are Programmed to Fail 53

FOUR

Define Your *Why* as Your Legacy 81

FIVE

Schedule Success or Live in Regret 101

SIX

Use a *GPS* for Vision and Values 127

SEVEN

Respect the Power of Ego in Accountability 157

EIGHT

Find Mentors, or Settle for "Good" 173

NINE

Discover the Dangers of Goal Myths 193

TEN

Practice the Nine Be's of Networking 211

ELEVEN

Embrace Uncertainty or Accept Complacency 231

TWELVE

Gain the Happiness Advantage 243

90-Day Massive Action Plan 263

About the Author 267

START HERE!

Massive Actions Become Mindful Habits

As you examine this book, you will notice that each chapter title is an action ... a *massive action* needed to develop your very own Success Psyche.

You'll start by learning why success is a snowflake, and it only gets more exciting from there. These twelve massive actions then become habits that you need to succeed both in business and in life as a whole.

Let each one become a part of how you live every single day.

Here's to cultivating your Success Psyche!

SUCCESS
PSYCHE

(noun):

A mindset, a philosophy, and a way of living that attracts your unique definition of success and allows you to be happy as long as you continue taking massive action.

Your Success Psyche is the lightbulb that won't dim. It's the part of your brain that is trained to view failure as progress.

WE SHOULD
NOT JUDGE PEOPLE
BY THEIR PEAK OF
EXCELLENCE, BUT BY THE
DISTANCE THEY HAVE
TRAVELED FROM THE
POINT WHERE
THEY STARTED.

HENRY WARD BEECHER

ONE

LEARN THAT SUCCESS IS A SNOWFLAKE

have a confession to make.

I'm a thief.

I stole most of what you are about to read. But I'm a thief with good intentions, I assure you. I have done nothing with the information except *execute* on everything I learned.

Are you surprised by that?

You really shouldn't be. At this point, we all know there is absolutely *nothing* new under the sun. Go online right now and search for books on success, and you'll find the options plentiful, confusing, exhausting, and repetitive.

Do this for any other topic—you'll get the same result. That's because the amount of information available to us is Never. Ending.

And yet, here you are, reading *my* thoughts on success. I'm humbled by that and the fact that you think you have anything to learn from me.

You are probably here because you've seen me speak, heard me on a podcast, or follow me on social media. That also means I know why *you're* here: Something about me or my story resonated with you.

On the other hand, if you know nothing about me, this book will show you how a guy who used to flip eggs and hash browns at Waffle House figured out a system for creating something extraordinary.

My secret? It's actually not a secret or even that complicated. And I plan to reveal it all in the pages that follow.

Yes, I really do promise to "reveal it all." There is no bait-and-switch here, where I give you a few morsels, and you have to pay $999 for my online course to learn the rest. I tell people that if you do what I do, you will be as successful as you want to be.

I can say this, knowing full well that 99 percent of people will stop short of achieving their personal definition of success simply because they will not execute.

But I'm not here for them.

I'm here for you—that one percent that really cares. You are part of that one percent ready to do the work that will lead to success every single time.

Here's the thing. If you are getting excited right now, you *already* have the critical components that make up the Success Psyche. I hope you find encouragement in that, but, if not, let me repeat it:

You already have what you need to be successful.

I'm just going to help you put the pieces together and show you how to make it all work to lead you down a clear path that has eluded you up until now. Here is how I know you have what it takes: I'm *just like you*—except I'm probably less educated. I dropped out of college and never went back. I made mistake after mistake.

And yet, here I am.

Somehow and some way, I'm now the kind of guy who gets asked, "How'd you do it?" I'm used to hearing daily questions from people about my businesses and my processes, questions like:

- What makes you tick?
- How did you get to where you are now?
- What got you through the tough times?
- How do you deal with setbacks?

These are all great questions, but the unfortunate thing is this type of questioning also does a disservice to a person's journey as a whole. There is no way to answer these questions in a few brief sentences that paint a complete picture of the struggles, failures, and setbacks that each victory represents.

Broad-brush stroke, "How'd-you-do-it?"-style questions paint a totally incomplete picture of success.

The truth of the matter is that success—like a snowflake—is *never* the same twice.

Not only can success never look exactly the same for two people, but it's also so easy for us as human beings to trivialize the success of others. It's natural for us to look at the big success stories in life and think:

- Wow, it must have been so easy for them.
- They've got natural talent.
- They had a leg up in life.
- They got lucky.

Pick any excuse for minimizing another person's success … it doesn't matter. What excuses like this don't take into account is this: The fame and wealth of people like Michael Jordan and Jeff Bezos happened because of *all* the things we will never see or fully understand.

We didn't see their journey. We only come to know these success stories when all the hard work got cashed in and the benefits of years of sacrifice and pain and sweat were realized. We didn't see the work and hours and failures that got them to where they are today.

It's the same for me. My colleagues, team, and connections see me now and want me to quickly impart a few Confucius-like proverbs that will make their path to success shorter, more comfortable, and less painful.

They don't know (or maybe don't want to know) all of the trials and tribulations I experienced.

They have no idea that I once lived in my car.

They don't have any concept of my childhood or what experiences from my past have affected my present.

They don't realize that I used to operate Waffle Houses for a living and work ninety hours a week. Not the most glamorous of jobs.

They don't know that I served in the U.S. Air Force and was deployed to Dhahran, Saudi Arabia, during Desert Shield.

Everyone just sees the Jay Adkins I am now, but he was a long work in progress and still has a long way to go—believe me.

Within the last few years, even after I had achieved all that I *thought* meant success to me, I kept having epiphanies.

And one of them is what led to this book.

LET'S CUT THE FLUFF

At a Tony Robbins event in early 2020, I learned something surprising about myself. Tony asked the crowd a seemingly straightforward question, but it wasn't easy to answer at all, at least not for me.

He asked us, "What do you do, and what do you *really* do?"

It may sound hard to believe, but I'd genuinely never thought about it that way.

What do I really do?

During that event, I started to figure out that what I *thought* I did (grow businesses, train sales teams, blah, blah, blah) and what I *really* did were not the same.

At the event, I was able to influence and lead many of my fellow attendees as the acting "CEO" of our group. We ended up winning first place in a contest where Tony challenged all 2,500 of us from 53 different countries to see who could create the most successful business idea in 72 hours.

In a life filled with other prominent business successes, this relatively minor win was a watershed moment for me. I inspired a group of people I had never met before, and it dawned on me that my expertise and experiences positively impacted many people in an exciting and tangible way.

The ironic part is that I felt more inspired than ever before when I realized that I was inspiring others. That is when it hit me—my *real* work is to impact people's lives.

If you think that sounds corny or cliché, that's okay. We live in a society now where the only messages that seem to resonate sound like "rise and grind" and "10X or die, bro!"

I do think it's essential to "grind" when you are at work, but my purpose in writing this book is to help you gain the right mindset for success on *your own* terms, not mine.

- Maybe you could "2X" your life and be successful.
- Maybe you need to figure out how to prioritize your health over a TV addiction.

- Maybe you have some bad habits that have kept you from a game-changing promotion.
- What if you made just 30 percent more than you do right now?
- What if you made the same amount you already do but found a job that you actually looked forward to every day?
- What if you were able to spend more time with your kids and spouse?
- What if you found a career that enabled you to work from a yacht?
- What if you were able to retire at 50 instead of 65 (or never)?

There are so many different definitions of success.

Find yours—and then I want to help you get there.

I also promise you this: If I can do it, then anybody can. I don't have an Ivy League education. I don't have impressive degrees. I doubt my IQ is special. I just outwork other people, I'm highly coachable, and I'm willing to do things that make me uncomfortable.

> **I plan to challenge you throughout this book to do things that make you uncomfortable.**

I also want you to know that just by reading this book, you are already doing what I do *habitually*. Whenever I come across someone really successful, I stop, watch, and learn. I also ask as many questions as they'll let me ask, and if they get tired of answering my questions, I'll pay them to tell me more (whether in the form of a book, coaching, or teaching).

Each of us should be doing the same thing if we want to do more and feel that sense of satisfaction from knowing that we set goals and did whatever it took to reach them.

I learned many of the ideas in this book from asking the most successful people I know question after question. I always make sure to ask them about their failures—because anyone alive for more than a few minutes knows that the most valuable lessons come from failure.

I told you from the first sentence that I've never invented a new strategy out of thin air. I will not be introducing any earth-shattering philosophies that will be brand new to you.

What I *have* done is effectively combine the "best of the best" ideas, philosophies, mindsets, and strategies and assembled them all here in one place.

So, consider this a shortcut past the fluff. The end result is a **GPS** that leads to the kind of daily successes that are attainable, repeatable, and available to every last person who is willing to put in the work.

I know you are anxious to start learning how to cultivate your Success Psyche, so let's dive right into the first step toward getting the most out of the great "success" stories. And the secret is to know more about them than just their end results (i.e., their apparent successes in life).

Listening to a guy in a suit on a stage lecture from a PowerPoint presentation is fine, and you may pick up a thing or two from him. But listening to another person's story and understanding what they went through to be qualified to *stand* on that stage—now *that* is when you've got the potential not to just learn, but to *transform*.

That is my goal for you—that you will become genuinely transformed by reading this book.

I JUST WANTED THREE STRIPES

I grew up with two parents who barely made enough to pay bills and never considered doing anything about it. We could leave it at that, but I want to paint a more complete picture. I want you to fully understand that no matter what did or didn't happen to you when you were a kid, you don't have to let your childhood define you.

My father was a former Marine who could *not* let that military background go and believed himself to be my lifelong drill instructor. The end result was a childhood that was controlled and stifled.

There was no room at all for outside-the-box thinking.

My dad had his way, and that was the only way in our house. That was an unfortunate trait when it came to our relationship because it just so happened that I wasn't a fan of submitting to authorities for the sake of it.

The end result was that I was always challenging him. Challenging his ideas. Challenging his preconceived notions of what was and was not acceptable.

Even at a young age, I knew that our financial state resulted from my father being unwilling to get a little uncomfortable and push himself. We were always down to our last dollar, and I knew why. I knew some people scratched and clawed their way to success, and then there was everyone else—the excuse-makers.

I also figured out that I didn't want to be like my dad at a really young age. I know how that sounds, and I mean no disrespect to my father. To this day, I'll tell anyone who asks that my dad *absolutely* gave me the single greatest gift that life has ever given me:

> *My dad showed me what life would be like when you don't consistently set goals or don't put yourself in uncomfortable situations.*

I promise you that insight was a *gift* that enabled me to be who I am today.

My dad did the best he knew how to do. No parent is given a handbook at the hospital when their kid is born that spells out the perfect way to raise a child. Sorry, but you have to figure it out for yourself, and let's be honest—some moms and dads figure it out a little bit faster and more successfully than others.

I choose to be grateful for the lessons my dad accidentally taught me rather than focus solely on his perceived failures as a parent.

Discomfort is what makes you grow anyway.

My mother loved me unconditionally, but she didn't know what she didn't know, either. She worked hard all her life as a hospital housekeeper, cleaning up after sick people. Even after working thirty years at the hospital, her salary was barely enough to pay the bills.

Suffice it to say, we were not swimming in extra cash. The most common phrase in my house was, "We don't have the money for that."

This fact never actually bothered me until I was twelve years old. That was when everything changed.

It was the year when the bullying began—and let me tell you that getting bullied makes you question everything you thought you knew, and it also makes you grow up quickly.

My classmates started making fun of the clothes and shoes I wore. Instead of sporting the Levi's and Jordache brand jeans that my classmates had, my jeans were Rustler brand from K-Mart. I also wore generic, no-name shoes (the kids called them Bobos) from K-Mart that were supposed to look like Adidas shoes, but they had four stripes instead of three.

An extra stripe? No big deal … until it is.

> I'd like to say I didn't let it bother me.
> But c'mon. I was twelve.

I couldn't have cared less about stuff like that until I realized other kids did. Once I started getting bullied, all bets were off, and I was determined to stop the harassment and wear what the popular kids wore.

Kids can be pretty cruel.

Pretty soon, they also started making fun of my lunch. My dad would pack me a peanut butter and bologna sandwich in a brown paper bag. By lunchtime, I was stuck with a warm, soggy peanut butter and bologna sandwich, all because he didn't want to pay 60 cents a day for school lunch.

I used to throw that nasty thing in the garbage rather than face the ridicule. I just wanted to eat pizza, chicken nuggets, and Salisbury steaks like everyone else.

Around the same time, all the kids my age started going to the roller-skating rink every Friday night, but that required money, too. It cost $7 to skate, and, as you can guess, when I asked my dad, his answer was always, "We don't have the money for that."

So, I decided to fix my problems. That started a lifelong habit of responding to difficulties by working *through* them rather than running away from them or playing the victim card.

Even as a pre-teen, I knew there had to be a solution. So, twelve-year-old me went into problem-solving mode.

First, I negotiated with my aunt and grandparents to mow their yards for $7 a week. In the wintertime in Ohio, where the weather was harsh and cold, that turned into cash every time it snowed because I'd walk around and shovel snow off the sidewalks for a fee.

Next, I got a paper route. I started delivering papers every morning, and I hired my brother as my first employee. I paid him 25 percent of the profits even though he did half the route. Sure, he delivered half and *technically* deserved equal pay, but he was younger. My "older brother logic" led me to conclude he only deserved 25 percent.

The day came when I could buy my very own Jordache jeans and even a pair of Levi's 501s. I could also afford some Nike sneakers, but I wasn't making enough to buy the current season's styles and bought the "cheap" Nikes instead.

To my disappointment, I still got bullied because I didn't have the most up-to-date style.

So, I decided I needed to earn even *more,* and I heard that golf caddies made good money. At this point, I was 13 years old and knew nothing about the game of golf—but that didn't stop me. I went to caddy school and, shortly after that, started caddying for doctors and lawyers. I made $10 an hour, which was more than my dad made, and I also kept up my paper route.

But I wanted more. So, at 14, I negotiated with the owner of a local Italian restaurant to hire me even though I wasn't old enough to work for pay. I went back daily for three weeks and asked him to hire me. "I can do anything a 16-year-old can do," I assured him.

Finally, I told him I'd work for free, just to show him that I was worthy. He could tell I wasn't going to give up, so he finally relented, "I'll tell you what. I'll hire you as a dishwasher. Just make sure you stay in the back."

I worked hard and won the approval of the kitchen staff, wait staff, and management. Eventually, I was promoted to busboy and started getting a part of the tip pool.

Anytime I wasn't in school or at the skating rink, I was working. I worked at the restaurant, caddied on the golf course, or delivered my paper route.

I was making good money, and I loved it, mainly because it meant that I didn't have to ask my father for a dime. It also meant I no longer had to hear the phrase I'd grown to dread: "We don't have the money for that."

From age twelve on, I provided for myself. I bought my own clothes, my own lunch, my first car, my car insurance, my everything. I craved freedom, I wanted to fit in, and I preferred nice things—and money provided those things for me.

> **I had found a driving force that compelled me.**
> **I had taken control of my life, and it felt good.**

Even though I wanted to play basketball in high school, I weighed the pros and cons and decided working was more important than playing a sport that would never pay the bills. Was I good enough to get a scholarship? Probably not. Was I ever going to be a professional basketball player? Highly doubtful. But I sure as heck could get a jump start on college tuition and save up for a nicer car, brand name shoes, and a motorcycle.

The message here is not "it's all about the money." For me, earning money was the simplest way to solve the issues I had encountered so far in my short life. I saw a way out of being ridiculed and feeling dissatisfied, and I saw a way to get what I thought I wanted. I found a way.

There is *always* a way. That is what I learned during my childhood. I happen to think that is a critical lesson! Would I have learned that lesson if my father made more money or was less controlling? Maybe, maybe not. Either way, I'm grateful for him because he inadvertently taught me to be relentless—to find a way.

Out of these experiences came the emergence of my entrepreneurial spirit, and it only blossomed from there.

YOUR COUNTRY HAS CALLED

I never doubted for a second that college was the next step in the path for me. That's just what people do, right? You graduate high school, and then you go to college.

The problem was that I was used to earning good money, but the demands of my first semester of college did not allow me the time to work a 50- to 60-hour workweek.

Halfway into my second semester, I knew this arrangement was not going to work for me. That's when I decided to give the Air Force a try. The idea of becoming a pilot was appealing, and I would be able to put in fewer hours of actual work time and still make decent money. Not to mention that when you enlist in active duty, you can get your tuition paid. That sounded good to me, too.

While I never regretted my choice to join the Air Force, a few issues arose because of this decision. First, I realized that it was hard for people with entrepreneurial spirits like me to accept the concept of getting paid the same amount no matter how hard I worked.

> **Up until that point, it was always "work more hours, make more money." Not anymore.**

It also didn't matter how hard I worked when it came to promotions. I worked harder than everyone else, but advancements were awarded by time and grade, not effort. That led to an overall mentality of "do just enough," and most of my fellow airmen refused to do any more than the bare minimum.

I was in for another surprise in 1994 when I got deployed to Dhahran, Saudi Arabia. I had just 48 hours to wrap my head around the idea of leaving the only country I'd ever known. I was a full-time student and also worked full-time. Surely, they didn't actually expect me to walk away from school and my income?

I'll never forget when we heard the news. It was a Sunday. Our commanding officer (whose last name was also Adkins) explained that we were being deployed as a part of Operation Desert Shield to help patrol the Kuwaiti border.

I was stunned, but I collected myself, raised my hand, and said, "Lieutenant Colonel Adkins, Airman First Class Adkins, permission to speak."

"Yes, Airman Adkins, what can I help you with?"

I proceeded with caution. "I'm in the middle of my semester, so I'm assuming that I'm going to join you guys after the semester finishes. I'll just fly over and join you, correct?"

Lieutenant Colonel Adkins was swift with his reply. "Airman First Class Adkins, your country has called. You will be on a plane with the rest of your squadron in 48 hours."

I was still confused or maybe just unwilling to accept reality, so I raised my hand again. "Yes?" my commanding officer said, this time with less patience in his voice.

"But Lieutenant Colonel, you told me you supported me and really wanted me to become a pilot. This is going to mess all that up."

He didn't miss a beat. "Airman First Class Adkins, your country has called. That's why you joined the military. You will be on that plane in 48 hours."

As unpatriotic as this sounds, at that moment, my heart sank in my chest, and I was devastated. I loved my country, but I had fought tooth and nail for the last eight years to take control of my life, and now that control was suddenly being stripped away.

Lieutenant Colonel Adkins was right—I was on that plane 48 hours later. For the next nine months, I worked twelve-hour shifts in a tent in the desert, seven days a week. None of us even knew what was going on because airmen first class weren't kept in the loop. Knowledge was *way* above our pay grade.

I was determined to get back home alive and find a way to regain control of my future. I soon learned that if you find another government job that pays you a third more than you are currently earning, the military could release you.

That's when I discovered the state highway patrol, and I immediately applied to be a part of the program. I took the tests and got accepted after an exhaustive background check process. As a result, I was released from the military five months early.

So, this was it. I was going to be a state highway patrol officer. Did it matter that I would have a career where the income was based on a salary rather than the "work more, make more" mentality that was more in my comfort zone?

Nope. The highway patrol represented a way for me to take control of my life and get back to the states. They let me out, sent me home, and I had six months to start the academy.

EGGS, GRITS, AND EXHAUSTION

When I told my father that I planned to become a state highway patrol officer, he was surprised. "That's harder than Marine Corps basic training," he told me, possibly somewhat impressed.

This actually made me want to do it even more. My dad had been so disappointed that I joined the Air Force instead of the Marines. I figured maybe this would be a way to prove my grit to my dad in a language that he would understand.

The highway patrol training program was over six months long, with a 70 percent washout rate. I wanted to be ready, so I enrolled in Basic Law Enforcement Training, or BLET, in Fayetteville, North Carolina. It was a shorter program that would give me the fundamental skills I'd need to excel in the more rigorous highway patrol program.

A week or so before I started the basic training, I ran into a good friend at the mall I hadn't seen since before I left for Saudi Arabia. Back then, when military personnel got deployed overseas, no one really knew about it except for family and maybe a few close friends. There were no cell phones, no social media. My only communication tool at the time was a rotary phone with a 30-foot-long cord.

So, this friend, like most of my other friends, had no clue where I'd gone. All he knew was he used to see me every week (we raced motorcycles together), and then, all of a sudden, he didn't see me anymore.

My friend came running up to me, "Dude, what happened to you?"

"Oh, hey. Yeah, I got deployed to Dhahran, Saudi Arabia."

"Wow."

I shrugged and asked my friend, "What are you doing now?"

"I'm working at Waffle House," he replied.

There was no way I could have hidden my complete surprise. "Waffle House? Why in the world are you working at Waffle House?"

He explained, "Man, I'm a manager trainee. They're paying me like sixty grand a year to train as a manager, and then they're going to give me my own restaurant."

I laughed. "I don't care if I got paid a million dollars a year. I would never work at Waffle House!"

Unfazed, my friend asked me to do him a favor. "Can you come interview? I have to recruit people, and it would make me look great if a guy like you comes in."

I was not even remotely interested. "Listen, I would never want to work in a restaurant again. I hated it when I was a kid. There is no amount of money they could offer me that could tempt me."

Somehow, despite all my protests, I agreed to do the interview and showed up the next day in a suit and tie to be interviewed by a district manager named Len. He had two earrings, a gold chain, and long hair. I was *so* unimpressed—me, with my super-shiny shoes, super-short haircut, and fresh out of the military.

After fifteen minutes, I'd had enough. I was polite but told Len the job just wasn't for me. "I've got to be honest. Looking around the restaurant … yeah, not something I want to do."

"Alright, man, it was a pleasure meeting you."

I rose to leave but in walked two executives from the corporate office. They stopped me as I tried to make my escape, "Excuse me, are you Jay Adkins?"

I nodded, and they continued, "Oh, are you already done with your interview?"

"Guys, this is just not for me." I turned toward the door again to leave.

"Jay, do you play golf?" one of them asked me.

"Yeah, I love golf."

"Good. Let's go play a round."

Being poor at the time, I wasn't about to turn down a free round of golf.

The following morning, again, I found myself in a place I'd swore I'd never be. An ironically large cook named Tiny was teaching me the best techniques for flipping eggs behind the grill at a Waffle House.

Tiny slapped some white stuff on the plate, and I marveled, "Wow, so people eat mashed potatoes with eggs for breakfast here?"

Tiny looked at me like I was crazy. "Boy, those ain't mashed potatoes. Those is grits."

"What's a grit?" I asked.

It was like the twilight zone for me, but I told myself I would work there just until I started the highway patrol program. My new employers were going to pay me $65,000 a year—and, at 21 years old, that's a formidable sum of money to turn down.

By my calculations, I would end up making close to $35,000 during those six months and then start the program. But then the guys at Waffle House corporate sweetened the deal. They offered me an $80,000 salary and my own restaurant in Wilmington, North Carolina—right on the Atlantic Ocean.

I called the highway patrol and told them I couldn't pass up on the opportunity. They understood, and I took off to Wilmington to enjoy the sandy beaches and my new salary.

I was going to be living the high life!

Well, it turns out I never saw the beach a single time. I worked ninety hours a week in my restaurant and only saw the outside of a Waffle House long enough to sleep for a few brief hours, shower, and shave—and then do it all over again.

Four and a half years later, I ran multiple restaurants in North Carolina, working on hours a week, 365 days a year. I made close to $150,000 a year by this point, but given all the hours I worked, it honestly wasn't even close to worth it.

I was miserable, but I kept my head down and did the work. I was the "golden child," so to speak, and I knew they were grooming me to help run the whole company one day. It was never because I was the smartest. I just outworked everybody, I had the right mindset, and I was extremely coachable.

One Friday night, on my first weekend off in years, I went to my best friend's birthday party and met a guy who worked for New York Life. His description of the work and the pay intrigued me, but I wasn't ready to jump just yet.

A few months later, I went on vacation, and as each day went by, I was dreading going back to work. By the following Monday, I couldn't force myself to get out of bed. I could sense then that my mind and body were ready for something completely different.

I called the guy from the party and asked if we could meet to discuss the New York Life opportunity. By the end of the meeting, he offered to pay for my license and get me started.

So, I called my boss at Waffle House and told a lie. I said I was sick and needed a few days off. It almost broke me because I despised lying and instantly felt like karma would make me sick.

My boss made me feel worse by being so gracious about it. "Listen, man, you've never taken time off. You don't even use your vacation days. Do what you got to do. We'll get it covered."

I drove to Charlotte, North Carolina, and took the licensing course, and on the last night, our class wanted to go to Waffle House of all places to eat.

C'mon! Really? Waffle House?

I was so conflicted. Was this a sign that I was doing the wrong thing? Was I walking away from the opportunity of a lifetime just to go sell insurance?

My inner turmoil was at a breaking point as our class walked into the Waffle House that night. As I looked around, it was the dirtiest restaurant I'd ever seen in my life. I felt disgusted on a cellular level.

At that moment, the universe was sending me a clear message: "Take it all in … because *this* is what you represent."

I decided right then and there that I wasn't going to work for Waffle House anymore.

I'm not one to keep secrets, so on the way back into town, I met my boss at a gas station Subway and handed him my two-month resignation. He'd never been given a two-month resignation notice before, but I felt it was the right thing to do. I knew I had a significant role, and they'd need time to find my replacement.

I also wanted to be there to make sure they hired a worthy successor. I'd poured my blood, sweat, and tears into that job, and I wanted to leave it the right way.

He tried his best to convince me to stay. He was persistent, but there was no offer and no amount of money that could have persuaded me (and this time, I really meant it).

I wanted to make sure I was crystal clear, so I told him, "I'm not staying. This is not my destiny. This is not what I want to do for a living. I *hate* this job."

He looked genuinely shocked for a moment and then replied, "Dang, boy, you need to go to Hollywood!"

"What are you talking about?" I asked, annoyed and confused.

"No, I'm serious. You need to go to Hollywood because you're a good actor. If you asked me to name who hated their job of all the people in this company, you'd a been the last person I'd guess."

I was glad to hear this because I worked hard and had tremendous pride in what I had done and helped build.

> **I've never done just enough. And I'm definitely not a "phone it in" kind of guy.**

I told my soon-to-be-former boss, "Listen, I have several hundred people working for me. If they see me sweat my job, my life's going to be torture. If they see that I hate what I do every day, they aren't going to show up and do their jobs."

But he sure was right about one thing. I did have to go into "actor" mode every single day for over four years. Every minute I had worked for Waffle House had been a struggle. Dealing with the different personalities and lifestyles that just didn't click with mine, the 24-hour shifts, the grueling 365-days-a-year schedule, the Christmas shift every year that lasted from 4:30 a.m. until 1 a.m. the following morning.

There was a lot to dislike.

But I also will tell you this: The entire experience made me appreciate my life so much from that moment forward. I've never had a schedule quite like that since, and even remembering it now makes me appreciate how good life can be.

I appreciate the freedom that I have. I appreciate the weekends. I enjoy being able to play with my daughter on a random Monday morning just because. I love going to lunch with my wife when she surprises me at the office.

Life is a gift, and sometimes it takes a few years at Waffle House to realize how good life really is, with or without grits, three-striped shoes, or Jordache jeans.

SET THE RIGHT EXPECTATIONS

There's more to my story (we haven't even gotten to the part where I lived in my car), and we'll get there, but this book isn't meant to be an autobiography. You paid money for this content, which means you are entitled to have some expectations.

I simply wanted to give you a good picture of who I am and who I am not.

In fact, there are just two times you can have expectations from anyone in life. You can have expectations whenever you pay someone money for something because that is a contract. And you can have expectations for your own self.

And that's it.

If you reach the end of this book and don't feel like I held up my end of the bargain, feel free to reach out to me on social media and let me know exactly how I let you down. I'll refund whatever you paid for this book. Also know that if you do this, I'm going to ask you if you get equally upset with yourself for not living up to your *own* expectations.

- Do you quietly set goals for your life and your business and then watch them go unfulfilled with no repercussions?
- Do you promise yourself you will get up at a specific time in the morning and then hit snooze day after day?
- Do you promise your family you will make more time for them, but then busywork … and email … and social media … and blah, blah, blah?
- Do you promise yourself you'll hit a certain income amount but never sit down with a pen and paper and reverse engineer the numbers to figure out how?
- Do you get on the scale and vow to lose weight but then eat a doughnut for breakfast and fast food for lunch?

I could go on and on, couldn't I?

Most of us break promises to ourselves every single day.

That ends with this book. I am going to show you how to hold yourself and *no one else* accountable for *your* success. I can't physically do the work for you, but I can give you the mental tools and the knowledge you need to make it happen.

Do you know how to set an expectation and actually hold yourself accountable? It's not that complicated, but it may make you uncomfortable. Well, get used to uncomfortable—because being comfortable is the greatest enemy of success.

Another enemy of success is your ego. Unfortunately, battling your egocentric tendencies (and we *all* have them ... every single one of us) is a lifelong fight. The good news is recognizing when your ego is getting in the way is half the battle.

It's also essential to learn how to *tame* your ego because that will allow you to remain coachable.

> **If you can be coached, you can win.**
> **That's all there is to it.**

I tell everyone who asks me about my success that it's never been about my education or my IQ (since both are nothing special). *If you want nice stuff, you've got to work for it.* I understood that by age twelve, and it's just as accurate today as it was back then.

We will get into the psyche of a successful mind, one that sees obstacles not as roadblocks but as *puzzles* waiting to be solved. One that sees failures not as disasters but as vital and necessary *lessons*.

I hope to help you understand the difference between reaching for goals and chasing the idea of success (the key lies in your focus). You have three options for focus—past, present, and future—and only one of them is the right focus that leads to success.

I also want you to know the difference between *chasing* success and *living in* success. People who chase success never reach it. There is always a bigger house and a nicer car, and I'm sorry to break it to you, but someone will always have more money than you.

To have a Success Psyche, you have to understand that success rests in actively pursuing your goals. Just by taking one step in the right direction and doing something you are committed to doing, you are successful.

Celebrate those "micro" successes because they are everything! You have to have the big goals, and you have to set a plan in motion, but when you say, "This is what success looks like for me," you also have to remind yourself that you won't get there by tomorrow. You won't get there by next month. And depending on the goal, you may not get there for years.

> **What are you going to do today to stay the course and maybe even advance down the road?**

If you're continually chasing some ultimate, *I'm going to be happy when* … finite point in the future, you are going to live an absolutely miserable existence. You've got to find happiness *today* for what you've accomplished *today* because that's going to give you fuel to complete what you need to accomplish *tomorrow*.

We'll talk about how to make a morning routine that sets you up for success and how to get past the harsh truth that the world has programmed us to expect to fail. With every success comes failure. When one area of life is going well, another may be falling apart.

Winston Churchill once said, "Success is walking from failure to failure with no loss of enthusiasm." Before you turn the page and continue on in this book, I want you to find that enthusiasm for challenges and get ready to learn lessons from failure.

Are you happy with the life that you have? If not, this is no one's fault but yours. Choose to approach this journey with joy and determine that you will find a way to achieve success every day. Waking up five minutes earlier is a success. Working out in the morning is a success. Making that extra sales call when you are tired is a success.

Did you know that no matter what you do for a living or how much money you have right now, you can feel fulfillment? I'm not telling you to settle. But I am asking you to "settle in" to the life you currently have to find the good in it.

Deciding every day that you will be happy doesn't mean that you're going to stay where you are. Still, it's absolutely the only way to enjoy the journey and be more enjoyable for the people who are journeying alongside you.

Set your sights on that more significant success you want, but bring that focus back to the present moment—and then start getting used to feeling a little uncomfortable.

Name the cliché; they're all true. The early bird gets the worm … take the stairs … the point is that winners do things that other people aren't willing to do. They get uncomfortable every single day.

Usain Bolt didn't magically wake up one day and become the fastest man in the world. Jeff Bezos wasn't born with the business plan for Amazon taped to his baby crib. The end result—the big success stories—all involve countless steps we never saw.

Don't forget that as you turn the page and continue this journey. The Success Psyche is not a final destination. We'll learn more about it, one element at a time, and each step is a success all on its own.

I CAN TEACH ANYBODY HOW TO GET WHAT THEY WANT OUT OF LIFE. THE PROBLEM IS THAT I CAN'T FIND ANYBODY WHO CAN TELL ME WHAT THEY WANT.

MARK TWAIN

TWO

OUTLINE YOUR TERMS OF SUCCESS

Do you know what you want? I mean, do you really *know*?

I ask every person in my life the same question: "If you could wave a magic wand and the perfect dollar amount could appear in your bank account every month, what would that figure be?"

I ask them to define the amount they would be content to make monthly—the amount that would make them feel like they have finally "arrived" in life.

The crazy thing is that very few people can actually answer this question. This is true over and over again, and yet it still surprises me every time.

What number pops into your head? Where did you get that number from and do you know what it would take to get there? How many hours a week would you need to work? How many clients would you need to see or how many products would you need to sell? What would you need to change about your life to get to that number every month?

And then the next question is this: Are you willing to do what it would take?

You don't have to have the answer to all of these questions right now, but I want you to start thinking this way.

This chapter is all about defining success on *your* terms, not someone else's. Later in the book, I'll teach you how to break down your goals in a way that gives you a "GPS" that will lead you to the finish line each and every time.

But, for now, start figuring out what that magic number is as we talk about one of my greatest childhood heroes.

THE LAST DANCE

Anyone else a Michael Jordan fan?

If you are, you may have seen the documentary *The Last Dance* on Netflix. The highlights of the full ten hours are too many to mention, but regarding *success* and how the world defines it, the show really hit me hard.

Thanks to the series, I discovered a lot more about one of my childhood idols. When I was a kid, I looked at MJ's fame and thought, "Wow, he is so lucky to have all those adoring fans." As it turns out, the mass recognition was the part that he liked the least. You could even say he hated it.

For Jordan, there always seemed to be someone digging around for gossip. People love to stir the pot—to turn greatness into negativity by unearthing a scandal or trying to invent one. They see success and conclude there *must* be some shocking problem with this person because no one can "have it all."

That is true in a sense. There is always an ugly underbelly, an untold story, a dark side. It's because we're human, and, frankly, we should be giving each other a lot more grace than we do. But, for some reason, that's not how life works.

The way we're always looking for "chinks in the armor" of others also got me thinking about how quickly we assume how another person's success makes them feel. I was 100 percent *sure* that Michael loved his adoring fans and the constant attention. But the fact is, we have no idea how someone thinks about their own success.

Does their success even make them happy?

And what happens if that success fades away one day?

That's another thing about success—it never seems to be permanent. This is definitely true for professional athletes. After they retire, the mentality for many becomes, *Well, what do I do now?* For players like MJ who lived for the game, it can be a long and lonely road.

Kobe Bryant is a shining example of an athlete who transitioned from his glory days in sports into another kind of success. After he retired from basketball, Bryant invested himself into his kids and seemed to love every minute of it. Before his life was tragically cut short, he found a way to evolve from one definition of success to another.

I'm only recently discovering how incredibly rare that transition is. Most people connect their entire identity to a static definition of success that lives in their heads. When that definition can no longer be achieved, the results are often catastrophic.

Success is becoming more and more complicated by the minute, isn't it? In reality, I don't think success is that complicated—at least it shouldn't be when it's properly framed and understood. Let's keep going.

SOMEONE ELSE'S DEFINITION

There's no doubt Michael Jordan was born to play the game, and he had an insatiable desire to be the best. Playing basketball and playing it well—that was his dream. However, having the spotlight thrust upon him was not something that he ever wanted or enjoyed.

He didn't want to be anybody's idol. He just wanted to play. He loved competing and winning, but he didn't want to be put under a microscope.

I know someone out there is probably thinking, *Well, that's the price you pay for fame and fortune.* If that's the case, I guess you better be careful what you wish for. It's yet another reason why it never pays to chase another person's success. Pursue your own!

Thanks to social media, there are so many success types that it's hard to choose which one we want to chase. Do you want to be like the coaching guru, the reality star, the makeup mogul, the real estate tycoon, the pop diva, the pro athlete, the outspoken actor, the investor shark, or the TikTok star?

I would hope most people understand that online, all we see is what people want us to see. It's all a show. There may be an "authentic" post from time to time (maybe a *#nofilter* selfie here and there), but we all know it's a façade.

C'mon, we're not idiots.

But here's the crazy part: Because our eyes are programmed to process what they see as real, our brain subconsciously starts to think that everyone's lives are, in fact, the perfect way they appear. The really harmful part about that is that we then begin to believe something is wrong with our own lives since our truth looks nothing like what we see online.

The programming is deep, and it's only getting more intense. That's why you need a Success Psyche now more than ever. The process of developing a Success Psyche is essentially the same for everyone. No person on this planet can achieve their personal definition of success—and do it well and sustainably—without taking some form of the twelve massive action steps in this book.

However, the result is going to look vastly different for everyone.

Some people want to be billionaires. Some people want to make half a million dollars a year. Some people want to work fifteen hours a week and have freedom. Some people want to be artists and don't care about money.

In 2020, my *Success Paradigm* podcast co-host Greg Gray and I interviewed Pulitzer Prize winner Dr. Jericho Brown. Dr. Brown has earned about as many accolades as a writer can achieve. He has all the right degrees. Still, money has never been his drive. His ultimate goal is to be recognized as an artist who impacts people's lives through his craft.

That's why we wanted to interview him in the first place because, believe it or not, money is not a driver for every successful person. Motivation and success gurus would have you think otherwise, but it's true. If you want to try an interesting experiment to test this idea, here you go:

> *First, ask people what the "definition of success" is. I predict most will respond with how they think society defines success (as in money, early retirement, big house, nice car, lavish vacations, etc.).*
>
> *Then ask them again, and this time emphasize that you want to hear their "own personal definition of success." I predict one of two things will happen:*
>
> *One group of people will have no idea what their personal definition of success is. They'll hesitate before answering, and it will be apparent that they've never stopped to think about success on their terms.*
>
> *But for the other group, you'll see their eyes soften. They may even look away as they talk about wanting to be there more for their family, growing old with their spouse, or being able to help send their kids to college.*

This is what really matters to our fellow humans, not their bank accounts or their Instagram followers. And yet, people have been programmed to answer the success question based on what other people think or what they believe they are *supposed* to believe.

It's like they're trying to live out someone else's definition of success.

People do this so quickly, almost without thinking. That's because it's so tricky to undo childhood programming. Little girls see a performance by Beyoncé and think, *Wow, what an amazing show! I want to be just like her one day.* They don't think about the amount of time invested into choreography, practice, wardrobes, and more, just for that one show—all the unseen effort.

So, those little girls grow up, and when the sacrifices start to get tough, they "settle" for less, and then the comparisons begin. *I guess I'll never be as successful as she is.*

Will you never be as successful? Really? By who's standards, exactly?

Let's think about Beyoncé's *actual* life for a moment:

Beyoncé works out daily with her personal trainer, and her nutritionist plans every last bite of food that touches her lips. She's vegan and doesn't eat carbs or drink alcohol. She has admitted that she is always hungry (people like Beyoncé do not eat until they are full). She does crazy amounts of cardio and sings in the shower for twenty minutes every morning to clear her sinus passages as a part of keeping her voice healthy. We haven't even begun to touch on her beauty routine—the skincare, the procedures, the treatments, the hair, and the makeup.

Add to this the many days, weeks, and months she spends away from her family and from her children. She can take them along with her, but if she rehearses fifteen hours a day, that doesn't leave much free time. We see pictures of celebrities like Beyoncé and Jay Z on vacation and think they live this lavish, relaxed lifestyle. Yes, some moments are first-class. Just don't forget the other 330-plus days.

Sound excellent to you? If so, maybe you've got what it takes to be a superstar. If not, you are probably like most of us in that your definition of success looks a little more "basic" (at least according to *US Weekly* or *Forbes*).

> It's time to create a new picture of happiness and success. Your own.

If you want to be the next Beyoncé or Elon Musk or Michael Jordan, that's great. You just need to be prepared for the sacrifices and then be honest with yourself about whose dream it really is you're chasing.

THE DECISIONS ARE YOURS

No matter how big or small your success dream, I guarantee it will do one thing: Dreams bring ridicule. People are going to try to rain on your parade. You will have haters. Friends will tell you that you are not smart enough or capable enough. It almost doesn't even matter what your goal is—someone will say to you that you can't.

Artists and aspiring actors experience this every day of their lives. What's the running joke? If you're an "actor in Hollywood," you're probably also a "restaurant server in Hollywood." That's what the world wants us to believe—that if we strive for our dreams, we will crash and burn and eventually be forced to settle. The programming conveys, without words, that if you aim high, you are going to be disappointed.

You aren't going to get far if you care about what other people think. The only person who should be able to judge your definition of success is you. But that won't stop other people from judging you.

Not even your mom or dad should have the right to tell you that you can or cannot pursue a goal. If you take the steps in this book and know what it's going to take, your parents don't have the right to stop you.

> **Living for your parents is not a satisfying way to live anyway.**

As a part of the process, you will have to decide who determines the lines you won't cross (in other words, what sacrifices you aren't willing to make). If you are single, the only person who gets a say is you. If you are married with a family, they should probably have a voice since your life decisions significantly affect them.

At more than one point in my career, I have worked 80-plus hours a week. I've been asked many times if it's necessary to grind that hard-to-reach pinnacle heights. Do I really think it is an essential ingredient?

I don't have a universal answer to that that applies to everyone, so I'll say this: People can be born with natural talent, but the misconception is that those talents somehow "naturally" make them successful. That's not how it works. There are no shortcuts to lasting success—ever.

It takes 10,000 hours to become great at anything, so you have to invest insane amounts of time in becoming great (even in things that seem to come "naturally" to you). You can become *good*, but the prodigies, the musicians, and the Tom Brady and Serena Williams-level professionals invest daily into their craft. No exceptions.

I still put in an 80-hour week, but that looks entirely different today. Thanks to my morning routine that you'll read about soon, I now spend close to 20 hours alone each week on myself before I ever interact with the world or my clients and colleagues. My businesses get a large amount of my time, but never close to 80 hours a week anymore.

When you're running that type of schedule, you live for your work instead of your work living for you. Just don't forget the personal growth time, no matter your age or life circumstance. Read books that will make you grow, and take care of your body, mind, and spirit. You'll be a better businessperson, entrepreneur, parent, spouse, and human.

There is no such thing as an easy road to success. There *is* low-hanging fruit, and there are isolated incidences of fleeting success. But to have stabilized success, you have to put in the time. Don't misinterpret this as me telling you that you have to work 80-plus hours a week. Just understand that if your goals are lofty enough, you're going to have to outwork everyone else. This takes patience and planning to do it right so that your efforts are focused and not frantic.

Our instant gratification society has destroyed patience, and the need for immediate results is wreaking havoc on happiness as well. Technology is a primary enforcer of that mentality because everything is at our fingertips—literally at the push of a button. The most unfortunate side effect of this is that people now believe there is an *easy* button for everything.

If you want something lofty, it will require sacrifices. For example, my wife Ximena decided in 2019, after a career transition from film and television into entrepreneurship, that she wanted to retire within five years. So, she began working 14-hour days growing her business. Within seven months, she was number one in her company.

If her time frame had not been so limited, those long hours might not have been necessary. Still, she wanted to make enough in the next five years to never need to work again—unless she wanted to. Will she actually stop working? Probably not. It's not how she's wired, and it's one of the reasons why we work so well together because I'm the same way.

The takeaway here is simple:

> **Unless you define your success, you will not be able to shape your life in a way that leads you there.**

I don't have all the answers, and neither does this book. Your success and my success are going to look very different. But I do know that if you take the massive action steps in this book, you will be far down the road toward your most significant accomplishments.

DO THE STEPS

There are plenty of books that you can read to acquire the knowledge you need to successfully pursue a specific goal. There are courses and coaches available to help you. The opportunity is there for every single person living in this country. But it doesn't really matter if you aren't willing to do the hard work.

Because that's the key—*willingness*.

Are you willing to sacrifice comfort, sacrifice doing things that you want to do, and instead do painful things?

Let's say you know the pain and trials that come with a particular goal, but you want it anyway. That's a commendable first step, but don't stop there. Whatever your definition is, you'd better make sure you think through what it will take to get there and decide if it's worth it to you.

The process of cultivating your definition of success and pursuing it takes planning. There are dreams, and then there are goals (more on that later), and if I was going to present a quick-and-dirty guide to defining your success and basing plans around it, here's what it would be ....

Step 1: Envision it.

If you had a magic wand and could magically transform your life into anything you wanted it to be, what would it look like? Picture you at your happiest. What types of things or people are around you? What work are you doing? Are you traveling? Are you coaching others? Make sure you don't think of anyone else's life as you are envisioning your own.

Does your success definition include family, career, hobbies, work-life balance, fame, time freedom, financial freedom, or traveling? Do you want to retire? You certainly don't have to (it's just another societal construct). Show me the rule that says it's all bingo, *Judge Judy*, and shuffleboard after age 65.

Now imagine being old one day and looking back on your life. What things need to happen to ensure you don't feel the sting of regret? What actions or missteps do you need to avoid? I'd like you to write down your definition of success now, and then you'll do it again at the end of the book.

_____

_____

_____

_____

_____

By the time you reach the end of the book, you're going to see if your success definition stayed the same. Once you've discovered the critical action steps needed, what are you going to do about it?

Step 2: Reverse engineer it.

The next step is one of the hardest things you will ever do. You have to do some "reverse engineering" to figure out what it will take to get there. What actions and sacrifices are required? What will make you uncomfortable?

One of the best ways to think through a goal is to talk to someone who has already reached the level of success you want to achieve in an area. Ask them for a detailed breakdown of how they got there. And don't expect anything for free—pay them for their time. People who have put in the hard work deserve to be compensated for their time, knowledge, and experience.

Another critical part of the reverse engineering piece that many people miss is figuring out what you need to *avoid*. What do I need to do for success, but also what do I *not* need to do? What common mistakes must I avoid? It might be spending money too much money before you have it. It might be making sure that you always remember where you came from. It might be making sure that you treat people the way that you want to be treated.

Step 3: Ask the big question.

After you know what it's going to take, that is when you make the big decision, the critical decision: Are you *willing* to do whatever is necessary to achieve that goal? Assess your level of willingness before you continue. Don't skip this step.

Step 4: Set a date.

There are clichés about goals and how hard they are to achieve, but the easiest way to say it is this: A goal without a deadline is a dream that will never live outside your head. Then one day, it will become a continual source of regret. We'll talk a lot more about this in Chapter Six.

Step 5: Let it loose outside your head.

When it comes to the massive things in life, don't make the same mistake so many do. Don't keep your goals inside. Tell other people because you are a *terrible* accountability partner for yourself. You simply cannot do it alone. There are things that you need to know, and there are people who already have the answers. Find them. More on this later.

SUCCESS BEGINS WITH YOUR FEET

Some people are consumed by the trials they face. Others are built by them.

Michael Jordan never allowed the fires or controversies stop him from reaching his goals and even beyond. In fact, all massively successful people share a common experience: *Their greatest triumphs come after their greatest mistakes.* How do those rare individuals turn tragedy into triumph?

It's actually simple: The champions in life stand back up and keep moving forward. That means that success is fundamentally about our feet. Yes, our *feet.* Athletes certainly know this.

To this day, you've never gotten anywhere without them. Your feet get you out of bed in the morning. They take you to work every day. And they walk you down the aisle: political aisle, church aisle, grocery store aisle. Your feet take you everywhere.

They are the unsung heroes of your life.

If you've ever met me, you know that I love three things almost more than anything else. First, I love systems and processes. Second, I love the way that sports and athletes like Jordan provide the perfect analogies for business. Third, I love acronyms.

So, I came up with an acronym that represents the four rules that get me through life and onto the next objective. These work hand-in-hand with my core values that you'll read more about in Chapter Six. Here are the four heartfelt principles (or the FEET) upon which I have built my life and my businesses.

Fun

Don't be content with dull, monotonous work. Be willing to work hard (harder than most), but that work better be fun, too! Having fun makes work feel less like a J.O.B. and more like a dream career—the kind where you have to pinch yourself to remember it's real.

Excellence

Everything you should do and everyone you choose to work with must strive for excellence. That's not some buzzword—it is the goal of every interaction and every customer experience that I first learned from my grandfather. Excellence differentiates you in a world where everything is starting to look and sound exactly the same.

That could be the way you dress, the way you manage, or the way you talk to people. One of my least favorite words is "good" because *good* is the antithesis of *excellence*. I don't ever want to associate my name or reputation with anything that is "okay" or "good enough." I'm always looking for excellence.

Evolution

You're either growing or you're dying. Resolve to stay humble, teachable, and ready to reach new heights every single day. I'll never believe I've reached the "top." Being alive means there is room for improvement. This is another lesson that I learned from my dad. He's always been stuck in his old ways, and, for the most part, his inability to change with the times has kept him stuck in the past.

I don't ever want my kids to know more than me. I want to be doing what they're doing, to be constantly up-to-date with trends and technology. I work to stay up-to-date with current events and politics. It matters because those news stories affect my life and business decisions.

Think about this: Just a little over a decade ago, most people still had flip phones and were pressing the "1" button three times just to get to the letter "C" in order to text their friend. That wasn't that long ago.

Life changes quickly, and you've got to be ready to change with it.

Trust

People do business with other people they like, know, and trust. Strive to leave your customers, colleagues, and friends all better off for knowing you. They need to know they can trust you to do everything you promise—and then some. Become the kind of person who over-delivers.

You also have to trust that failing is just part of the process. You have to trust that it is going to be hard along the way. You have to trust that the work you're doing and the commitment you have to follow through on your word is just a part of the process.

Notice I did not say the process is perfect. That's where your feet come in yet again! If something is not working in your life or business, you can fix it. You have the power to stand up, turn around, and walk in a different direction.

There's always more to learn, always new mistakes to be made.

But take heart: Real growth comes *through* those mistakes. I've learned the most important lessons through trial and error. I've encountered huge obstacles and made horrible decisions. I've focused on the bottom line. I've been too focused on results and not enough on people. I've been selfish and narrow-minded.

You can't look *at* someone's success but *behind* it. That's where you'll gain an understanding of the path it took to get where they are today. You'll find it was no straight road but a jagged journey of tough lessons and bad choices—a journey we all walk using our FEET.

BE LIKE YOU

My idea of success is loving what I do every single day. As cliché as it sounds, my work is not truly "work" to me. There are some monotonous parts to what I do, but I don't focus on the minutia of doing a job well. I focus on the satisfaction of the end result. I also want to impact lives and change mindsets. This is becoming more and more important to me every day.

I'm at a place in my life where I can choose what fulfills me, and that's a success. Money is an essential measuring stick because it proves that what I'm doing is working. I have people around me that I like to be around. Heck, I even look forward to meetings with my staff and to my weekly podcast. I'm building a life of things that I wake up and look forward to doing.

I mentioned my wife earlier, and it's relevant to point out that she and I have different life goals. We also share goals as a family, but, individually, Ximena and I have our own dreams. Don't miss this:

> **You need a distinctive success definition from that of your spouse or partner.**

While we're being honest about marriage and individual goals, let's also cut to the chase regarding another elephant in the room: Most people don't finish books.

I'd like you to challenge yourself to finish this one (if you enjoy what you're reading and feel it's worth your time). You need all the massive action steps for the best possible chance at developing a Success Psyche that transforms your life. Give yourself the highest odds for achievement. Do the hard work, and do it every day.

If you start books but never finish them, that's indicative of how you approach life. Regret lives within most people because they never finish what they start. So, digest this book from beginning to end.

As we continue this process, repeatedly ask yourself: What does success look like for me, and what will I do to create it?

Here's a secret: It doesn't take that much more than what you're already doing to find success. If you understand the necessary steps, you are *already* better off than most people (not that "most people" is ever a good benchmark). If you increase your productivity by as little as 10 percent, I predict you will find yourself skyrocketing toward your goal.

I remember a 1990s Gatorade commercial featuring Michael Jordan. It showed images of MJ playing basketball and laughing, as the song in the background crooned, "Sometimes I dream that he is me ... like Mike, if I could be like Mike."

I understand the thought (and I have fond memories of that commercial), but a better message for kids might be this:

| **Define success on your terms and be like YOU.**

Why would you want to be anyone else? That sounds exhausting and unfulfilling.

Michael Jordan was a competitor, and in everything he did, he wanted to win. He was willing to do whatever it took to get to that level, and so he put up with the fame that came with it. All the greats in the world want to win, and they have a passion for what they're doing.

You can admire these traits and aspire to develop them as well, but it's got to be on your own terms, or it's not going to work.

Without passion, discipline, consistency, and a uniquely chosen path, you'll always be living in regret. You'll always look at other people and say, "I wish that I could be like them."

There's already a Michael Jordan in this world. As incredible as he is, we don't need another one. We need you—and your original contributions. So, I'd like to invite you to start figuring out exactly what those are and what kind of mark you want to leave on the world as we continue.

IF YOU ARE
AFRAID OF FAILURE,
YOU DON'T
DESERVE TO BE
SUCCESSFUL.

CHARLES BARKLEY

THREE

REALIZE YOU ARE PROGRAMMED TO FAIL

This chapter title may not seem to fit in a book about success, but stay with me.

Before I explain how we are all programmed to fail, why it matters, and what you can do about it, let's talk about one of my favorite books of all time.

The most popular books become that way for a reason. Generally, that means it is because they have changed enough people's lives that those people can't help but tell others. One of the books that have withstood the rise and fall of countless other fads in the success and motivation genre is *The Power of Now* by Eckhart Tolle.

The title says it all—there is immense power in the here and now. This, by default, means that our strength does not exist anywhere else but in the present moment.

> **There is absolutely no power for us that lies
> in the past.**

We are powerless to change a single thing that has already happened. And yet, that is where so many of us live, because we exist in a state of *regret*.

Most people tend to live in regret. I've thought a lot about remaining in a constant state of guilt and what it means to a person's quality of life. I have spent many years living there myself. My mom passed away eight years ago, and for a period after her death, I felt the stinging pain of regret over not spending enough time with her and not being there for her as much as I should have been.

Plenty of people live with the regret of not spending more time with their kids and missing them grow up. Then the year 2020 came along and offered us all a chance to slow down and spend more time at home with the people who mean the most to us.

Some people went stir-crazy during the lockdown. For me, it was an unexpected gift during a challenging time. I got more face time with my daughter and stepson, I saw my wife more every day, and I made memories with my family—and I could *never* regret that.

Today, I despise the thought of taking an action (or *not* taking one) that would cause me to live in regret. In fact, my dislike of regret now fuels me, but it took me a while to get there. I had to experience it before I realized just how poisonous regret is to the present.

> **Some people live in the future—and those are the
> people whose driving force is *fear*.**

Fear may be an even more damaging emotion than regret. Fear causes people to run from their true callings, to avoid risks that could lead to success, and so much more. I have to admit that there have been times when I've let the fear of the unknown rob my present of its power.

Being present is the only way to create the brightest future for yourself and the people you impact most. The only way you can influence others is if you're fully present in the moment. The present moment is really the only thing you have right now that can be changed or affected in any way. Action doesn't happen in the past, and action doesn't take place in the future. Action happens now.

However, it's not easy to live in the present. Thanks to modern life and its pace, most people now live for and in the future. During conversations and interactions with others, we are already thinking about what we'll say next. We're thinking about dinner, about the next phone call, about the commute home, about all the "what-ifs" of life.

That is why, in whatever I'm doing, I do my best to make sure that every part of me is present and accounted for. When I am playing with my daughter or speaking with my wife, I'm there. I'm not on my phone, and I'm not thinking about what's next.

I'm all in.

I share this with my team regularly, especially now that it's even more true in the "new normal" workplace. We are not going to be face-to-face with customers nearly as often in the future of business. So, when you're on the phone with a customer, what they need more than ever is your presence. They need you to truly listen. They need you to be there for them.

What your family needs more than ever is your presence as well. They need you to know that you're there, you're strong, and you're paying attention to them.

FAILURE IS INEVITABLE

Living in the present is the central and critical piece to the Success Psyche. That means you need to start working on ways to stay grounded in the present—because the fight to the top of whatever mountain you are trying to climb is not going to be quick or easy. And the reason is because of this:

> **The world is expecting you to fail.**

The world expects you to admit defeat and trek on down that mountain with your tail tucked between your legs and fall back in line with the rest of the dissatisfied masses.

From childhood, we're programmed not to succeed but rather to give up after a failure. From naysayers to our own parents, those around us often unintentionally condition us to believe that we can't do certain things.

What is the most common word that toddlers hear?

NO.

No, you can't crawl there. No, you can't eat that. No, you can't get up yet. No, you can't have another one. No, you can't. No, no, no.

After childhood, our adult life is much the same.

No, that will never work. No, you can't do that. No, you don't have the right degree. No, you aren't good enough.

This negativity comes not just from the world around us but also from friends and family.

It's a type of programming that becomes so ingrained and so intrinsic that when you fail and someone says, "See, I told you that wouldn't work," you absolutely believe them and stop trying.

You believe they were right.

You give up and wonder why you ever tried at all.

Part of the problem here is the people with whom we choose to surround ourselves. You've heard it before, I'm sure, but it deserves repeating:

> **You must choose to spend time with people who you lift you up rather than tear you down.**

People who tear you down just want to feel better about themselves, and most of them are not even doing it deliberately. They're just miserable, and let's face it: Misery really does enjoy company … lots of company.

As human beings, we've always had classes, and we like it when the people around us fit into ours. You can witness the same thing in the animal kingdom because it's this innate thing we have inside us. We want to hang around with others who are like us.

> However, what we really should be doing is hanging around people who *aren't* like us.

The people around us should make us uncomfortable because that feeling of discomfort is the only way to undo the programming that failure is our inevitable conclusion.

The thing is, failure is actually inevitable, but there is more to the story. You fail, and you keep going. You fail, and you keep going. You fail, and you keep going. *Rinse and repeat.* But the moment you decide not to keep going—now, that is an *actual failure* that is never going away.

We battle our programming and the negative influences in our social and business circles all the time. It's a daily onslaught, and without the right Success Psyche on your side, the weight of the constant negativity and "no" mentality eventually triumphs.

Do not let that happen to you. Do not be a cautionary tale for your kids. Be the fish that's willing to swim upstream to get where you're going.

FAILURE CREATES LIGHT BULB MOMENTS

Failure is just a part of any standard process. Think about a child's first steps. Think about the first time you attempted a cartwheel. The first time you tried a new sport. Learning how to talk, how to ride a bike, how to parallel park, how to fly a kite.

Nothing important in this world is ever perfect or even close to right the first time around (or second time or third time).

Failure is as much a part of life as is love, heartache, happiness, and sadness. When you understand what failure is and recognize it as an essential part of progress, it instantly becomes something much less intimidating. Another game-changing realization about failure is this:

> **It is failure that brings about the "light bulb" moments in life.**

Edison failed a thousand times trying to perfect the light bulb. But he kept going. Because of his persistence, the world is now much brighter. (Granted, what Edison actually discovered after six thousand failures was not the light bulb itself but rather the right material for the light bulb filament, which was carbonized bamboo.)

Did you notice how many materials he tested? He tried six thousand possible materials. Without that kind of persistence through failure, we wouldn't even know the name Thomas Edison.

Without all the failures of great minds, we also wouldn't have things like automobiles.

We wouldn't have airplanes.

We wouldn't have the cotton gin.

We wouldn't have the Internet.

We wouldn't even have computers.

At the premiere of Tesla's new futuristic vehicle, the Cybertruck, Elon Musk had the lead designer come out on stage and throw a steel ball at the window as Musk explained that the glass was shatterproof.

Well, a spiderweb of cracks appeared (both times he tried). That meant Musk did the rest of his presentation in front of two cracked windows—a physical reminder of his failure.

How embarrassing for Elon Musk, right?

He should have just quit right then and there!

Or … maybe not. Musk would never let a failure—even a huge, public one—slow this journey for a moment. That kind of determination helped Musk become the world's wealthiest person faster than anyone else ever has (with the most significant single-year wealth surge in history in 2020).

Now Musk says he's going to Mars, and frankly, I believe he'll make it there because that guy refuses to fail. In 2018, Musk told CBS he'd been sleeping on his factory floor during the production of his Tesla Model 3 because he worked so hard that he had no time to go home and shower.

Elon Musk made the decision that no matter what it takes, he's going to succeed. He is a person who has re-written his programming and refuses to look at failures as the end.

So, what do you want, and what are you willing to sacrifice? But more importantly, can you embrace failure? If you do not recognize this ingrained programming, you will be destined to allow failure to derail you and force you back down the mountain.

SUCCESS IS SUBJECTIVE

Discussing a powerhouse like Elon Musk gives me a perfect segue to bring up something else you need to understand.

Not everyone is willing to sleep on concrete to achieve their dreams, and not everyone wants to be famous, get rich, or travel to Mars.

And that's okay.

There are different levels of success. Your current level of success is not "wrong" or inadequate—unless you think it is. For some, what they have right now is already more than enough. For others, it's not.

> **Success isn't hitting the bullseye on the target.**
> **For some, it's hitting *anywhere* on the target.**

However, if you want to reach a new level of success, that's great, too. If you wish to attain another level of success, you need to choose to be around people who are already where you want to be, or even higher. You are never going to get to the next level by staying comfortable.

The most successful people I've ever known are perpetually uncomfortable. Don't mistakenly read that as unhappy or dissatisfied. They find joy in life, but they can also see beyond their current level and strive to reach it. And that "reach" to the next level? Sometimes it hurts a little (or a lot).

Most of people you'll encounter in this life have convinced themselves that they are fine right where they are because it's just easier that way.

I'm doing okay. I have a nice house and a car that runs. My kids are well fed and well dressed. We go to the beach once a year.

If you can say a statement like that and not an ounce of regret or dissatisfaction creeps into your mind, then maybe where you are really is enough for you. And if so, then you have reached the kind of comfort and satisfaction that very few others attain in this life.

However, suppose you are honest with yourself (and I can say this about you because you are reading this book). I predict it is probably not enough to settle for "just enough" or "okay." Your subconscious is telling you that you want more, but you have been suppressing it.

Am I talking about material, monetary success here? Yes and no. Financial success is the door that opens up all the others, but for some, all they really need to be happy is a roof over their head and their family by their side. I love my family and my home, too, but I'm the kind of person who wants to challenge myself to do more and stay uncomfortable.

Discomfort fuels me as much as my desire to not feel regret. However, a word of caution is needed before we go any further:

> **You need to make sure you are chasing your own definition of success, not someone else's.**

You must determine this before you go any further in this journey by defining what success looks like for you. If you are chasing the success that your brother, best friend, or that influencer on Instagram has, that will not work. Even if you achieve that definition of success by someone else's standards, something will always feel *off* about it.

It will always feel insincere. Unsatisfying. Empty.

It's also important to tell you that if you're like the rest of us, your definition of success could change by the day. You may read something inspiring and decide to reach for more. Someone else's success may be the spark that causes you to think bigger. You may start a family, and your whole world changes along with your priorities and goals.

No one can or should judge *your* personal definition of success. Only you can judge what success looks like to you: the money you want to save, the level of freedom you need in your career, the amount of time you spend with your family, and the people or causes you want to help. It's all up to you.

Just don't forget that while you are chasing that dream, that goal, that big success, you also have to live in the present moment.

This can be a tall order because goals are, by default, something that you want to accomplish *in the future*. There are also many unknowns, and, right now, you're traveling down one path. But something, someone, or some event may come along that teleports you onto another one with no warning.

You have to stay flexible. You also have to stay grounded to react to those unexpected events with *conscious clarity*. Remain in the present moment, ready to respond to any failure. I know … easier said than done, right? I never said any of this was easy, but it is entirely doable when you have a Success Psyche in place.

THE MYTH OF OVERNIGHT SUCCESS

There aren't many things in life that are absolute, but here is one of them: *If you don't fail, you can't succeed.* As paradoxical as that may sound, there really is no other way to attain the success you want. Once you fully understand and accept that, it then becomes a matter of trusting the process—and knowing that each failure is leading you closer to where you want to go.

You shouldn't *wait* for failure and *expect* to fail, but, undoubtedly, it's going to happen. The more you attempt, the more you're going to fail.

When I'm going about my day, if something I try doesn't work, I don't even call it failing anymore. I call it *learning*. It may seem like an unimportant adjustment, but it's a significant one because it allows me to instantly start viewing failures more positively.

When I fail, I learn exactly how not to do something the next time. I understand how to improve it, so it's not a matter of, *Oh, no! I failed*, but instead, *Oh, good! Now I know what corrections to make next.*

There is another mistake I see people make. When they fail, they move all the way to the other end of the spectrum and try something completely different. However, doing so may end up causing you to have to duplicate your efforts, and that's not something I enjoy. At all.

Thomas Edison didn't scrap the idea of a filament altogether. He just tried different materials. Edison would fail, and then he would change one little thing.

It's called a tweak.

Don't do a full 180-degree change when a ten-degree shift would have set you on the right course. Just make the tweaks necessary and get back to work. Become someone who reacts with detailed precision out of determination rather than sweeping changes made out of frustration.

Imagine a toddler trying to walk for the first time. She takes a small step forward and falls. Does she assume the problem is that her legs and feet don't work? Of course not. If you are skiing for the first time and keep falling, do you assume the skis are the problem? Obviously not. Yet, this is what so many of us are essentially doing when we make extensive changes in our businesses.

You need more minor pivots and fewer sweeping transformations.

When you're a kid and learn how to speak and read, it's a journey. It takes a long time to remember those sight words and even longer to internalize phonics and spelling rules. But for some reason, when we become adults, we expect to learn everything so quickly—to become "experts" overnight.

Life has not and will not ever work that way. So, if you are wired for instant gratification, there is not much I can do for you other than to say that it's time for you to remember how you learned to read. One word at a time. One sound at a time. Slow down and understand the process. Overnight successes only happen in the movies.

Malcolm Gladwell is a smart author who knows how to market his books. When I first picked up his book *Outliers*, I thought that I would learn how to become an outlier myself or at least discover the traits of an outlier. I wanted to know the "secrets" to become one of those people who just naturally attract success without effort.

Well, imagine my surprise when I read the entire book to learn that there is no such thing as an outlier. It takes around ten thousand hours to become great at anything. It doesn't matter where you were born, your IQ, or your amount of "natural" talent.

> **Before you become a smashing success, the expert, or the authority in anything, you must invest at least ten thousand hours in failing.**

The only real "outliers" are outliers in the sense that they keep going when they fail. Thanks to our instant gratification society's devastating effects, persistence through failure is the exception and not the norm today.

We're taught that the participation trophy is enough.

We're taught that it's okay to fail and just stay down.

If you want to be an outlier, let go of the ideas like becoming an overnight success, making fast money, and finding the best get-rich-quick schemes.

Modern society has sold us a bill of goods. We need to call their bluff and go back to what works, which is persistence.

WHEN YOU GET PUNCHED IN THE FACE

It's easy to talk about the concept of becoming an outlier because it sounds good. After all, who wouldn't want to be one of those who can always push past obstacles and keep on keeping on? But what if you don't just stumble or hit a roadblock?

What if, instead, you get punched in the face?

Some things in life are more challenging to overcome than others, upon which we can all agree. Businesses fail, loved ones get sick or worse, relationships end, accidents happen. There is so much uncertainty in life.

> The thing is, no matter how big or small the hit, you still only have two options: Stay down or get back up.

I've dealt with many blows in life, and although this next story is not one of the biggest ones, it was still a face-punch moment.

Five months before the 2020 lockdown, I lost one of my executives with no warning. It was a punch in the face during a time when everything around me (and the rest of the world) was becoming more uncertain.

Whenever I face those kinds of moments, I liken it to being inside a boxing ring in a heavyweight bout, and I just got punched in the face.

I went down to the mat and thought, *Okay, that hurts. What do I do next? Am I going to get up and fight, or am I going to give up and stay here?*

Here's the thing—I did lie on that mat for a moment because sometimes you *need* that moment. I was panicked, and I was upset. If I'd jumped back up too quickly, I would have felt dizzy and could have made a hasty decision out of fear.

In the middle of my wallowing, my wife popped into my office and asked, "Do you want to take a walk?"

No part of me wanted to go for a walk at that moment. I wanted to keep wallowing. But I did it anyway, and the craziest thing happened. Things started clicking in my head. I started focusing on my wife and daughter and not the emergency. The panic subsided, and the dizziness did, too.

That's when my brain started coming up with a plan rather than an emotional response.

I went into solution mode and made a counterintuitive change. I called up three of my most stellar team members and made them cry. Don't worry—they were good tears. I gave them all raises because losing my best employee reminded me that great team members don't come along often. So, when you find a good one, treat them how they deserve to be treated.

It took me getting knocked down to the mat to realize that I should be taking better care of the people who help create success in my life.

So, I was bloodied and bruised one minute, but the next, I was feeling grateful. I had three great team members whose loyalty became galvanized. We were *all* (myself included) inspired to work harder for each other.

Both successful and unsuccessful people wallow on the mat. The difference is that successful people wallow on the mat for a minute, but they get up and keep fighting—and fight smarter.

Getting punched in the face is an opportunity. It reminds you that maybe you let your guard down. It's then an opportunity to get creative and not just remain on defense but work on your offense. Sometimes, that process can take a day, but sometimes it may take weeks or months. Again, remember that there is no such thing as "instant results."

It could be a month. It could be six weeks. But there's always a reason that something happened. If you have a Success Psyche, you get punched in the face, and you make the best of it. You go down and come back up stronger, grateful for the learning opportunity, and appreciative of the reality check.

Life is so uncertain. On the morning that I lost my key executive, did I wake up thinking that I was about to lose that person? Of course not.

But then it happened, and it pushed me into panic mode, and I became future-focused. I was focused on all of the business I was going to lose. It was all about what I *thought* was going to happen. I was already trying to predict the future.

It reminded me that old habits can easily creep back into our lives if we aren't careful. Long ago (during my Waffle House days), I woke up every morning consumed by stress. From the moment my eyes would open, I'd imagine different scenarios playing out (most of them negative). It put me on the defensive and forced me to carry the weight of that stress throughout the day. Looking back, I feel like it took a couple of years off my life.

I eventually learned that I can't worry about the future because I am not a fortune teller. There is nothing certain in life. All I have to respond to is in this moment.

But that morning, when I lost my key player, I started trying to tell the future again. I tried to predict what would happen next like I was a meteorologist forecasting the weather or like I had a crystal ball, and the outlook wasn't so good.

The old me would have stayed there and acted out of fear of the future, but my Success Psyche saved me (along with my wife's suggestion to go for a walk). Instead of predicting worst-case-scenarios, I figured out how to use the present—the only place where I have any power—to take my business to the next level.

What do worry and future predictions give you? Besides insomnia, high blood pressure, and reduced quality of life, they provide you with nothing.

Yet, we are programmed to live in the future because why? Because that is what the people around us are doing. And you know what that means? It means, among other things, you may need to find a different group of people to call your tribe.

BECOME THE CEO OF YOUR LIFE

Not everyone wants to lead a company. In fact, very few people would even be interested in becoming the head of an organization. This may be because the failure programming instilled in us during our childhood prevents most people from even believing they have what it takes to inspire others.

I say if you want to start and lead a business, go for it. I love being the leader of my own business. But, frankly, I'm not concerned with making CEOs out of everyone in the traditional sense.

> **I believe that everyone on the planet should be the CEO of whatever role they play in life. In marriage. In parenthood. In relationships with friends and family.**

Do you know who is in control of your destiny? I'll give you a few hints: It's not your boss, your spouse, the government, your parents, or your kids.

It's you.

Whether you realize it or not, you are already the CEO of your life!

Don't wait on your friends or family to do things that create a Success Psyche within you. That's not how it works. CEOs take the initiative to make things happen. They are not *reactive*. They are *proactive*.

I'm the CEO of my kids. As their dad, I decide what time they go to bed, what foods they eat, and what shows they watch. As a good CEO who cares about those he leads, it also means that I have the responsibility to set my girls up to win, to give them the best possible advantages in life.

There is a lot of responsibility in that role—and if I don't fill it, who will? Should I just step aside and let society dictate my kids' lives? I have a feeling that wouldn't go well.

As a good CEO, I also practice what I preach. If I tell my kids that they can't hang out with a certain friend because he or she is not a good influence, I had better fiercely protect my own circle of influence. If I tell my kids to read more books to help their minds grow, I had better be reading every day. If I tell my kids to dress nicely and comb their hair before they leave the house, I had better look my best before I leave the house as well. They need to see that sleep is important, and I model that by going to bed early.

> **I have to be an example worthy of following.**

I don't care what your job title is—janitor, mom, network marketer, vice president, salesperson, clown car driver, executive assistant, part-time server. It doesn't matter. You can be the leader wherever you are. Here are a few other things I know about CEOs in life:

1. CEOs commit to win.

It's imperative to have the drive to win. This is what has propelled my success. I will say that I hate to lose more than I love to win. But I *love* to win! Develop a taste for victory and never settle for less.

2. CEOs protect their circle.

We all have heard that the five people you hang out with and the books you read will determine what your life looks like in five years. I'm here to tell you it's true. Do you think the best CEOs (from the CEOs of households to the CEOs of Fortune 500 companies) hang out with people who lack confidence and drive? Absolutely not. Most people are negative, and you need to run like Forrest Gump away from negativity. Here are some questions to ask yourself (I recommend you write these down):

- Who am I spending time with?
- What effects do these people have on my psyche?
- What are they reading?
- What do we talk about when we're together?
- Are they making me better?

How do you feel about these answers? Don't allow people to influence your life unless they also have a Success Psyche. Fiercely defend your time and who you spend it with, and also make sure you are always filling your mind with high-quality reading material.

> If you aren't already a member of a book club, I'd like to invite you to join mine. Just go to: www.*Facebook.com/NextLevelBookClub* to join.

3. CEOs value growth over comfort.

Resilience is a key ingredient that differentiates the pro athletes from the amateurs. It's also a key ingredient in creating a Success Psyche. When something doesn't go right, you know by now that most of our friends and family either live in the past (regret) or start to live in the future (fear). The way to overcome failure and become stronger because of it is to work through our problems in the present.

A victorious life is not designed to be comfortable. Discomfort is how you know you are headed the right direction. It helps when you decide to value consistent progress over some giant breakthrough moment. In other words, it's about consistency because that consistency will compound. We are a society of immediate results. Success doesn't work that way—at least it doesn't stay around that way.

4. CEOs are lifelong learners.

You can never read, study, or research too much. It has been said that someone who doesn't read is no better off than a person who can't read at all. But then you also need to take it that extra step. Take what you learn and apply it through immediate action.

Learning is the beginning of wealth, health, and happiness. And yet, after 21 or 22 years of age, formal learning stops. This means that most spend the last sixty years of their life without any more discernible learning or growth. The three best ways to learn are through:

- Reading books.
- Observing and asking lots of questions.
- Reflecting on your own experiences and learning from them.

5. CEOs always sleep enough.

The most important thing you can do for your mental and physical health and your psyche is to sleep seven to eight hours a night. I have heard plenty of successful people say things like, "I'll sleep when I die."

Well, I say if that's how you operate, you'll be dead a lot sooner than you planned. When you get adequate sleep, you are clear, focused, and energized. It's also easier to find happiness in the moment and not allow fatigue to cloud your judgment.

Getting enough sleep is the number one key to developing your Success Psyche. I'm not being dramatic here: It needs to become *the* top priority in your day. Sleep will keep you young, motivated, inspired, and sharp. I always say to myself, *If I'm rested, I'm unstoppable. But if I'm tired, I'm not as productive as I could be.*

Good sleep is a habit, and it's one you can start to develop *today.* Go to bed earlier and schedule your sleep like it's the most important goal every day—because it is.

> **Commit to sleeping seven to eight hours a night, no exceptions!**

6. CEOs dress to impress.

My grandfather always told me to be the best dressed person in the room. That was hard to do when I was wearing Rustler jeans and bobos as a kid—but, over the years, I made this an integral part of my life. As a professional, I use my clothes to my advantage. Wherever I go, people always ask me what I do, and that helps me introduce my business and meet more people.

No matter where I am, I consider myself to be on stage. If you work from home, get up early and put on some nice clothes. Commit to getting out of your pajamas before breakfast and see what it does to your psyche.

You just never know who you might meet that will change your life. What if you are on a plane and meet your next opportunity? Always look your best, and more opportunities will naturally flow to you.

> When you look your best, you feel your best,
> and you act your best—and then you are *at* your best.

7. CEOs don't "try."

I hate the word *try* (and I don't hate a lot of things). *Try* is not a committal word. It says, "I will give it a shot, but I'm not going all in because I don't believe I can make it happen." The words to use instead are *I will*. Don't try. Just commit to action.

8. CEOs never self-sabotage.

The only person in the way of the life of your dreams is *you*. So, don't miss that critical step of defining your *why*. You'll need it when times get tough. If you don't know where you are going, I promise you will end up somewhere you don't want to be. Your *why* will give you purpose. The right *why* will give you a reason to jump out of bed in the morning and crush the day.

In corporate America, there are so many layers of leadership. The managers have managers who have managers who have managers. The loop seems endless! The reason why businesses have to structure it this way is because people don't do their jobs. Most people refuse to look at themselves as the CEO of their job, no matter the title.

When you see yourself as the CEO, you don't need someone else to "manage" you. You can manage yourself. You take the initiative to build good habits. You read every day. You take care of your body. You get enough sleep. You listen to others. You do the things that leaders do!

That's how you become successful. *That's* how you seize opportunities when they come your way. CEOs from all walks of life and in every position under the sun are all in control of their own destiny.

SUCCESS IS A MOVING TARGET (AND THAT'S OKAY)

Your definition of success should change every single day.

Unforeseen learning opportunities are going to happen. All the time. That's life. You are going to fail at some point every day. That's life, too.

Maybe today, success looks like a day of complete rest and relaxation with friends or family. Then, tomorrow, success will be helping your team through a series of setbacks. The day after that, success means you got up at 5 a.m. to work out.

The list could go on and on. The point is to expand your definition of success.

> **Don't ever let success become a static or linear concept in your mind.**

In the pursuit of developing a Success Psyche, it's easy to become future-focused. There is no getting around that. The end result is that we end up *chasing* success instead of living in it.

While it's true that a Success Psyche requires you to have a plan and goals for the future, the fact remains that acting on them requires small, daily steps in the here and now. There is no magic lamp, and there is no fast-forward button on some giant life remote.

You can only accomplish one thing at a time. You have that bigger goal in your mind, but then you bring yourself back to the present moment and say, *This is what success looks like for me TODAY.*

Later in the book, we will talk about vision boards and how to do them correctly (because they are easy to mess up and are useless without a strategy behind them). For now, just remember that you are not going to wake up tomorrow having "reached success" as some sort of fixed dot on a map.

None of it's going to happen tomorrow. None of it's going to happen next month. So, what will you do today to move toward your goal (with the full knowledge and awareness that another goal waits beyond that one)?

If you're continually chasing the ultimate, *I'm going to be happy when ...* goalpost, you'll never get there. Plain and simple. That kind of thinking is garbage and will lead to a life of dissatisfaction.

You can succeed in some life areas and find some semblance of balance no matter how busy you are or how far you have left to travel.

You may not have as much time with your kids as you would like, but if those moments you do have are quality, then that is what matters. For example, tell me which one is better:

1. Be home all day with your kids but be on your phone the entire time.
2. Spend one hour playing outside with your kids with no phone and no interruptions.

It's a no-brainer.

Even fifteen minutes of quality time is better than an hour of distracted time.

I spend one to two hours every morning with my daughter. I feed her breakfast, watch a Disney show with her, and play with her. Whatever she needs at that moment, I'll joyfully do it. I'm all in for those precious minutes.

In that moment, that's a real success.

Am I making the money I want to make? Am I impacting enough lives? Am I donating enough to those in need?

Truthfully, the answer will probably always be no.

But you can't mistake that for failure. It should serve as motivation to keep going, to stretch yourself. That is the essence of the Success Psyche.

This chapter was meant to lay a bit of the groundwork we needed in order to discuss the what and why behind my daily routine. I hope you got something out of it, but if you only remember one or two things, let it be this:

Define success on *your* terms and continually make a plan for the future, but then work like crazy to stay within the power of the present moment.

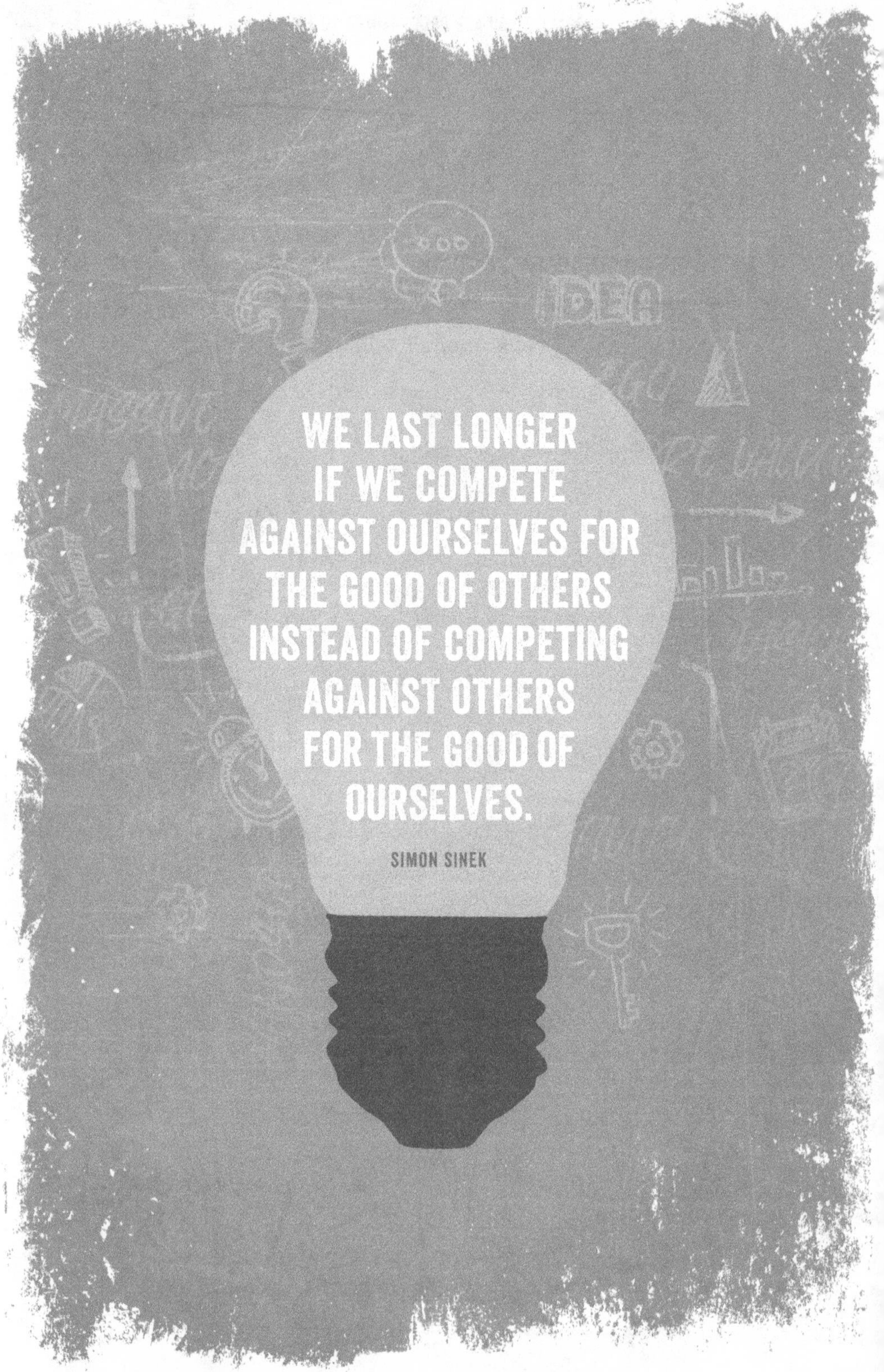
WE LAST LONGER
IF WE COMPETE
AGAINST OURSELVES FOR
THE GOOD OF OTHERS
INSTEAD OF COMPETING
AGAINST OTHERS
FOR THE GOOD OF
OURSELVES.
SIMON SINEK

FOUR

DEFINE YOUR *WHY* AS YOUR LEGACY

Ever since Simon Sinek's groundbreaking 2009 book, *Start with Why*, the business world has been inundated with discussions of the word *why* and what it means to our lives. If you haven't read his book, I highly recommend it.

When I began writing my own book, I also started with *why*. Ironically, as I started the process, I discovered that I felt compelled to write this book to *undo* some of the damage done by modern success gurus. Sinek's original message was filled with an unmistakable authenticity and truth. Still, since that time, many others have taken the idea and twisted it back into "start with profit."

When you break it down, there are only two ways to approach goal setting and journeying toward success:

1. You start with dissatisfaction and assume it's financially driven. When the going gets tough, you believe you aren't mean to have wealth or success and quit. You feel a sense of regret from day one of the journey.
2. You start with finding the why that will allow you to overcome the pain that accompanies change. You feel a sense of victory from day one of the journey.

Even before the *why* phenomenon, much success and motivation material focused on mindset as the fastest track to wealth. While this may be true for some, the concept has left more than a few people dissatisfied and wondering where things went wrong.

As a part of my Success Psyche training, I teach that money is an entirely optional byproduct of finding your *why*. Still, if financial success is what you're after, finding your *why* is the only path to get where you need to go.

Do you know why you want to be successful? If you don't have a *why*, you're going to quit when times get tough. I guarantee this.

In fact, I would go so far as to say that the absolute *most straight-forward way* to fail is to start without your *why*. A lot of people know this. However, they've also been programmed to fail, and they believe they will ultimately crash and burn. And they don't want to be held accountable to their *why* when this happens.

When you find your *real* and unmistakable *why*, it becomes the reason you need to jump out of bed every single morning. Without your *why*, your head fills with excuses and, more crucially, *justifications* for why you should just stay under the covers.

Your *why* is also what enables you to see failure as progress. One thing every successful person has in common is that they are not after what works ....

Successful people are looking for what *doesn't* work.

On the surface, that doesn't make sense. However, if you're going to be successful, retrain your brain to lead with this thought: *Let me find what doesn't work.*

Then, when you fail (and you will fail a lot), that failure will be its own kind of success because you have not failed. You have only found something else blocking your path that you can move out of the way.

When you focus on your *why*, it allows you to reframe failure as progress. It also allows you to see others' mistakes as learning opportunities. That way, instead of learning only from your own mistakes, you can shorten the "fail window." It's like condensing the success marathon from 26.2 miles to 13.1 miles.

RECONNECT WITH BELIEF

Speaking of learning from others' mistakes, those "others" definitely don't have all the answers. No one on this planet has all the answers. No one found the easy path to success that you can now copy step for step. To think that some people just "lucked" into success is just foolish. It's also a cop-out.

Don't sit around feeling sorry for yourself. Find a why that is compelling enough that you don't feel forced to hide behind it.

Unfortunately, when most people make mistakes, their innate failure programming and overriding "no" mentality causes them to be (dis)content to live in the past, always wondering what could have been. That is a game-changing mistake because if you're not moving on and correcting, you're not getting better.

It's all rooted in the way you look at failure, and this goes hand-in-hand with your opinion of yourself: *Do you believe you can accomplish anything?* Most of us have constant doubt that drives us to not take action because we don't believe that we can, or we don't even believe we deserve to win.

Remember when you were a little kid, and you believed that a fat guy in a red suit brought you presents every Christmas? Belief is magical. It can fill you with wonder and make you think that the impossible is, in fact, possible. That guy can fit into your chimney and even bring a ten-speed bike along with him.

Why does this magic die as you age? It's your failure programming, and you have to fight it with everything in you in order to override it. Ask any kid, and they'll tell you that belief makes things come true! You must believe that you can achieve what you set out to achieve.

If you believe that you're going to get sick … if you think you're going to get divorced … if you believe you're going to be late … if you think you're going to gain weight. It literally doesn't matter. If you convince your brain that something is real, your brain will find a way to make it real.

If you have a tendency to doubt yourself, you are up against a struggle, but the good news is I know you can overcome this programming. And the best way to overcome doubt and reconnect with your belief?

It's massive action.

FAILURE LEADS TO ACTION

People get knocked down and stay knocked down when they don't fight to change their programming. I was having a conversation with a client dating the same woman for over ten years. They also have a child together, and she desperately wants to get married, but he is not willing. I asked him why, and he responded, "It's just the way I was raised. My father taught me that marriage destroys good relationships."

I told him, "That's programming, and it's a lie. If you are damaged because of what you saw with your father, you can be the one to break the cycle of dysfunction."

Look, change is hard. It's comfortable to stay within our embedded belief systems. The idea of deviating from them is downright terrifying. But when we don't change, *that's* when we fail. I find myself saying the same thing to people I coach every day:

> **If you want to change your life, you have to change your way.**

You have to change how you think, how you do things, how you process failure, and how you process success. I included changing how you process success because I have seen time and time again that when people have even a little taste of success, they quit. They make the fatal mistake of concluding they have "arrived". Instead of taking your foot off the gas, you need to keep your foot on the pedal as you think, *Okay, great. Now, what do I do to shift to the next gear?*

If you're not failing, that means you're not doing big enough things. You can't become a master chef without burning some meals. You can't learn to ski without falling down. You can't become a pro basketball player without missing a lot of shots. You can't master a musical instrument without playing horrible notes.

Social media has done such damage to the Success Psyche. All we see online, day after day, are the shiny, perfect end results of an unspeakable amount of ugly effort and painful struggle. We see all of the money shots—the fancy homes, the cars, the piles of cash.

Remember, that glory represents mountains of massive failure. Don't forget the defeat. You need it. Why? Because defeat and failure are necessary to elicit three responses in you:

1. Failure should make you hungrier.
2. Failure should make you grow.
3. Failure should make you stronger.

The real secret is this: If a perceived failure doesn't make you grow, then you didn't actually fail—because when you have the Success Psyche, real failure always makes you act.

Do you have to immediately get back up on the horse and try again? No. You can give yourself time to process the failure and figure out its driving forces. There is nothing wrong with taking the time to process. Just don't confuse time for processing with a justification for giving up.

> **The longer you wait to get back on the horse, the harder it will be to make that climb.**

When I fail, I give myself some time ... but not much. I'm no different than you in that the self-talk kicks in, and I think, *Jay, you're so stupid! How could you have done this?* I'm not afraid of the self-talk—I just recognize what it is, and then I shut it down as quickly as possible.

There are only two types of crises: ones that are real and ones we create. Thanks to the power of our minds, we can dramatically transform minor setbacks into outright tragedies.

We all know the difference between a real crisis and a perceived crisis at this point in the ball game. If you don't, it's time to learn. Perceived crises should take no more than a few hours to move past in your mind. Resolve to get past them and go into solution mode. Real problems can earn a little more of your time to process.

The true mark of someone who has developed a Success Psyche is thriving during any crisis. Have you ever noticed that the biggest and best companies tend to be born during times of great turmoil in our country? Their leaders are people who recognize opportunities at every corner and learn how to use them to advance a collective *why*.

As long as a person's or a company's *why* is honorable, I see no problem with this. During the 2020 worldwide shutdown, many people panicked and immediately assumed their businesses would suffer or fail. I took the opportunity to completely take my team virtual and teach them how to *thrive* in a Zoom climate rather than just survive.

Every day, you should be reinventing yourself. This is especially true in a crisis.

Now, I have to admit that I wake up every morning with some level of anxiety to this day. It's hard for my ego to admit that because I know that anxiety and fear are *future-focused*. But here's what I also know: I know by the time I have half a cup of my coffee, and I'm halfway through my daily reading, I'm going to feel inspired and motivated.

I used to get frustrated by my negative self-talk, but now I'm empowered by it. I turned my frustration into a way to empower myself to understand that I want to get better.

Take it from me, the world's most extraordinary over-analyzer, that if you think about something for too long, you will become paralyzed. Overthinking is the enemy of progress. You need less wallowing and more action. The most massive action I take every day is reading for one hour. (You'll see how I make that a daily part of my life in the next chapter.)

One of the reasons people are hesitant to start moving again is that their failure programming taught them to believe that they ultimately don't have what it takes. I hear people say things like, "See? I just knew this wasn't going to work."

I shake my head when I hear this. The reason it didn't work is that you didn't think it would work! You self-sabotaged. As soon as you say these types of statements, they become self-fulfilling prophecies.

Think back to when you were learning how to ride a bike. Let's say you fell during that process and badly skinned your knee. If you are like most kids, that bike started to look a little scary and the thought of getting back on wasn't quite as appealing anymore.

If your parents were smart, they let you process that pain but, shortly after, they said to you, "Get back on the bike. Do it now, while you're afraid of it."

You didn't want to do it, and you may even have been mad at your parents for suggesting it. But your parents urged you again, "You're afraid, so now is the time. Show that bike who's boss. The only way you're ever going to conquer this is to conquer your fear."

Eventually, you got back on, and by the next day, you were riding around like it never happened.

Those are the types of things we forget when we're adults, but those same principles apply. It's crazy to me that we'll tell our kids every day to get back on and try again—to work past the pain and persevere—but, as adults, we never get back on that bike again.

We just lie there bleeding and admit defeat.

> **When you fall off your bike, you've got to get back on and keep pedaling.**

If you read other success books, you know all about the many failures of great men such as Michael Jordan, Abraham Lincoln,

Martin Luther King Jr., and countless others. Whatever you do, don't forget that you are not the lone victim of failure. Sorry, but you aren't that special. We all fail—every day.

If you're going to keep growing, failure is inevitable. Get comfortable with being uncomfortable with failure.

When Steve Jobs was alive and acting as Apple's visionary leader, their product development pace was mind-boggling. What started with a bulky computer and that chunky rectangle we called an iPod quickly became revolutionary products that captivated the world. Their products caused lines of people to be wrapped around electronics stores, breathlessly anticipating their release.

Who gets excited about a new iPhone now? What's it going to have —another camera lens? Boring.

What Apple has done since Steve Jobs' death is trivial by comparison. It's the same basic products. The technology now essentially looks the same, but it never looked the same when Jobs was alive.

To me, that's a massive failure. There's been no true evolution or giant creative spark. The people at Apple have gotten comfortable with their products. I predict that some creative dreamer will come along and sideline them with something revolutionary sooner rather than later. You can't take your foot off the gas and stay at the top. You just can't.

When it comes to your life, of course, there are no new products you can add to your lineup. That's why the way to make sweeping changes to your Success Psyche is actually counterintuitive.

> **You accomplish radical transformation by making small changes, day after day after day.**

If you don't think the minor details matter, you should read *The Compound Effect* by Darren Hardy. Sweeping changes and the significant events in life are the easiest to spot. Still, it's the daily "inconsequential" actions and "trivial" mindsets that make all the difference in the world to your outcomes and to your legacy. Every day, you can slowly whittle away at your marriage, at your health, at your business—at anything and everything that means something to your life.

Commit to becoming hyper-aware of the small things you are doing to sabotage yourself. Then, daily, commit to doing something that will move you toward one of your goals, even if it just makes you 1 percent better. (We haven't talked about the myths and misconceptions circulating about goals, so get ready for that later.)

There will be times when you're going to be tired, and that's when you need to go harder. Anyone can act when the ride is smooth.

Tired is a negative mindset and an excuse. *Tired* is something that you say when you don't want to take action. You have to be obsessed with feeding your mind positive thoughts. As you'll learn in the next chapter, that's why I don't read fiction books. When I take my valuable time to read, I pick something that will better me in some tangible way. Whatever you feed your mind with is what you will become.

> **You are what you eat, and you are also what you think.**

If you tell yourself every morning that you are tired, I guarantee that you're going to be tired every single day, no matter how much sleep you get. The Success Psyche requires you to act when the ride is rough or even after you've fallen off in mid-air. You've got to be willing to flex, pivot, shift, and change.

Just when I think I've got my morning routine all figured out (more on that later), my daughters remind me that the ride never stays smooth for long. I used to base my schedule around my oldest daughter's wake time. Then she started getting up earlier, so I had to shift.

Then we had a second daughter.

Fast forward ten, twenty, or thirty years down the road, and these adjustments will be necessary until the day I die. Nothing is certain except for the fact that everything changes.

Change with the changes, or get out of the way and live with regret.

VICTIMS RUIN IT FOR EVERYONE

Marriage is one of those areas in life where I see so much hurt and regret. It's also a topic I find myself discussing a lot (even in the business world) with others because there are so many damaged relationships and so much pain.

The reason is that marriage is one of the most challenging things that a person can do well. I love my wife, and she knows I feel this way. It's hard to be married because you go from being single and having one big ego to deal with to now suddenly having two. Add a few kids into the mix, and everything gets more complicated.

Humans are programmed to be self-centered. So, for a marriage to work, we have to force ourselves out of that place of ego and consider others' needs.

I know few people who are truly happy in their marriage. Most are honestly pretty miserable, and it's sad. One of the primary reasons is because people have a terrible tendency to make mountains out of molehills. I see this happening in marriages all the time, and it happens in our business lives as well.

We perceive a wrong (intentional or not), and the victim mentality sets in. That's the real killer because it leads to the dreaded r-word: *resentment*. Make no mistake—the victim mentality destroys marriages, and it also destroys businesses. It devastates lives, plain and simple.

> **Victims lie down and die, while people with a Success Psyche stand up and act.**

Marriage is an excellent reminder of how important it is to find your *why*. Without using your *why* as your compass in a marriage, your marriage is doomed to fail. Do you love each other enough to dig in and find what's not working and fix it? Do you love each other enough to set aside your ego and stop projecting and making up stories about how the other person may or may not feel?

If you can look at marriage this way, I believe it's even easier to do it in your business.

Your purpose in life, in marriage, in business, as a parent .... If it's authentic and genuine, that purpose should be able to light a fire in you and become the source that fuels you even when your damaging self-talk sends you into a tailspin.

Your self-talk has a funny way of contradicting your *why* and your purpose. That's why you have to get control of your psyche that tells damaging lies such as, *You are destined to fail, so why even try?*

One way to live in pursuit of your *why* and successfully ignore self-talk is to be intentional about your goals. I'll introduce the concept here, but rest assured you're going to see it again in this book. It's too important to miss.

Here's the gist: If you are living your *why*, you need to tell *everyone* what you are doing and what you plan to do. Then, you need to bring as many people on board as you can to hold you accountable. Even if you believe in yourself, if you keep that belief hidden inside, you will never develop the Success Psyche you need to fulfill your legacy.

> **Accountability is the magic ingredient, but it's also the one most people miss.**

I'll talk about accountability in more detail later, so get ready.

A lot of people are going to tell you it's not worth fighting for your goals. Plenty of people will tell you it's not possible. Don't listen to these people. They haven't found the strength to fight for what's possible, and they want others in their "regret camp" with them.

Don't go to the regret camp. It's a sad place.

These folks will try to convince you that it's not worth the sacrifice. But what they don't know is that when a goal is rooted in a genuine *why*, "sacrifices" don't even feel like actual sacrifices.

In case you haven't figured it out yet, success is not a finite place or a dot on a map. It's a mentality. It's a psyche. It's a state of mind. It's what allows you to move past the self-talk, the failures, the haters, and the setbacks and focus on this moment ... and then the next moment ... and then the one after that. Remember, the present moment is all you have to work with. So, when people tell you that you can't do something, you can respond in two ways:

1. You can believe them.
2. You can use it as fuel.

Whenever I hear people tell me I can't, I imagine a jet fuel truck pulling up to me and pumping more fuel right into my Success Psyche. These people serve a purpose in my life (to provide me with fuel). Still, it's worth noting that if you surround yourself with people who use the words "that's impossible," you're hanging out with the wrong people.

Never allow another human being to place a limit on you.

It's also worth noting that other people's threshold for sacrifices will be different from yours. No matter the number of sacrifices you are willing to make, just don't forget your *why*.

Why are you willing to make those sacrifices?

Does your family know those reasons?

If your spouse is giving you pushback because of your late hours, discuss your *why* as a family. Get them on board!

If work-life balance is a vital issue for you, you may never be an Elon Musk type who sleeps on the factory floor to get the new Tesla rolled out in time. That's more than okay. We don't need a world full of Elon Musks. We need more authentic people pursuing their snowflakes of success based on their unique *whys*.

I once heard someone say that there is always someone who wishes they were you. No matter where you are in your journey, I promise that someone else envies you. Don't forget that, particularly when you are tempted to start living in the past (a place of regret) or in the future (a place of fear). Live and work and exist in the present.

MAKE THE TIME TO STAND IN THE ARENA

When you find your *why*, the "there's not enough time" excuse goes away. It's like a beautiful, magic eraser.

We all have the same 24 hours in a day, and if we're being honest with ourselves, there's a whole lot of wasted time in our schedules. All that time scrolling on social media and watching TV? Waste. Now, it's not a waste if you already have enough time in your day to move toward your goals and spend time on other priorities (family, health, etc.).

However, if you think you can't put in extra hours because it would take away from your family, try logging off social media and spending that time with your kids. I imagine you'll have just as much time to work and also have made some lifelong memories in the process.

> **Get off the "loser's feed trough" that is social media, and take back control of your time.**

Does it take discipline? Absolutely. Again, that is where your *why* comes into play. You will not be able to do this unless you have started with *why*.

It's easy to recognize people who've found their *why*. They work harder than everyone else. They are rarely the most intelligent, but they can light up a room with enthusiasm and determination.

Find your *why*, and you almost instinctively develop a "whatever it takes" attitude. When I get knocked down, I will do whatever it takes to learn from that loss and get better. I step outside myself and that loss and realize that nothing I'm feeling is permanent. Taking myself outside the moment and objectively looking at the failure helps me move on more quickly.

The beautiful blessing in having a tough road to success is it makes the wins taste even sweeter. The low-hanging fruit is never as good as the good stuff that is out of reach.

You have to think about what you want your legacy to be, because guess what? Your legacy is your *why*! That type of mindset and the enthusiasm that comes with it will make up for any deficiency.

Don't have the right training or education? When you are focused on your *why*, you find a way. Don't have the solution or means? When you are focused on your *why*, you find a way.

Never forget that doubt is the worst enemy of determination. The people around us can be a huge source of that doubt, but it comes from within most of the time. You cannot be simultaneously doubtful and determined, so that means it's decision time: Which one is it going to be?

Are you going to let critics stop you in your tracks? What about your own self-talk? How about your lack of education? A physical ailment? Your height? Where you were born?

These are all the same—they are all justifications people have for accepting permanent failure (i.e., quitting) when they don't have a Success Psyche.

When we're kids, we want to be doctors, inventors, and astronauts. Then one day, that one adult tells you very few astronauts actually get to go to space, and most just sit behind a computer—and, from that day on, the dream slowly dies.

Stop the madness. Remove the word *impossible* from your vocabulary. Decide to define your *why*, and, by doing so, you will discover what your legacy can and should be. Then move heaven and earth to make it possible. Become someone who fails while daring greatly and who also triumphs. If you've never read this excerpt from the famous speech, "The Man in the Arena," by President Teddy Roosevelt, then you really need to:

> *It is not the critic who counts; not the man who points out how the strong man stumbles, or where the doer of deeds could have done them better. The credit belongs to the man who is actually in the arena, whose face is marred by dust and sweat and blood; who strives valiantly; who errs, who comes short again and again, because there is no effort without error and shortcoming; but who does actually strive to do*

the deeds; who knows great enthusiasms, the great devotions; who spends himself in a worthy cause; who at the best knows in the end the triumph of high achievement, and who at the worst, if he fails, at least fails while daring greatly, so that his place shall never be with those cold and timid souls who neither know victory nor defeat.

Who is fighting your battles for you in the arena? Who is in that Thunderdome with you? Is it your parents? How about your high school algebra teacher or your old baseball coach? Your boss? Your spouse? Your best friend?

None of them are fighting your battles. It's you. You're the one in the arena. So, keep taking massive action, and do it all with a *why*-led focus.

THINK IN
THE MORNING.
ACT IN THE NOON.
EAT IN THE EVENING.
SLEEP IN
THE NIGHT.

WILLIAM BLAKE

FIVE

SCHEDULE SUCCESS OR LIVE IN REGRET

hate getting up early in the morning.

I really do hate it. Yes, I know that's a strong word. But I mean it.

I would not call myself a morning person, and I've never been one. I could easily sleep until 10 a.m. every morning with no hesitation. I love my bed, I love sleeping next to my wife, and I love my pillow.

But you know what? I still do it. I get up at the crack of dawn, each and every morning. The reasons why I do it are not mysterious, and I'll explain them in this chapter.

I've sat on many panels and frequently hear this question: "What does your morning look like?" I've listened to other panelists answer this question, and while they say many things I agree with, what I usually hear are generalities. They say things like:

- I meditate to start the day.
- I work out in the morning.
- I get up early and read.

I do all of these things, too. But if I was new to the whole idea and wasn't sure where to begin, those generalities are honestly not that helpful. In this chapter, I'm going to break down the specifics of my morning routine. I am doing this not so you can copy it (though you are welcome to do so if you want), but so you can see how I map out my day and the *why* behind it.

I first learned about the importance of systems in the military. The number of systems and processes in place that enable our U.S. military to be a well-oiled machine is awe-inspiring. They instill discipline in you from the start, and I thrived on that discipline.

Early in my civilian life, I realized that I needed to have systems and processes inside of my daily routines that would create good habits. I believe a habit is really a system in place that makes your life better, more comfortable, more productive, or some other desirable payoff.

I needed to create a system that would set me up for the day and set me up for success the next day. The process of creating the system in this chapter was mostly trial and error. I continued trying different things to figure out what worked for me. I finally found a few elements I really liked, so I stuck with it and added new parts to the process from there.

The ironic thing about an elaborate morning routine is that while it seems selfish, the habits I have incorporated accentuate not only my life but also the lives of everyone I influence.

I am not just adhering to a schedule to "better myself." If I was doing it just for myself, it would feel insincere and empty. It would also be nearly impossible for me to keep up my routine seven days a week.

The ironic part comes in because it looks like I'm only focusing on myself. But when I focus on myself, I can be a better husband, a better father, a better coach/mentor, and a better friend because I'm in the right state of mind. I have the right Success Psyche to impact other people's lives positively.

If you are going to do something as monumental as changing the entire start to your day, you will need some guidance to get you started rather than some general advice.

It matters because of this: How you start and finish your day determines how the day in between is going to be. Period.

So, let's get started.

5:30 a.m.
Arise with Self-Talk

As I mentioned at the beginning of the chapter, I have never considered myself a morning person. When I wake up, I'm not one of those people who jumps out of bed spewing positive affirmations.

It'd be great if I were, but I'm not.

One thing I can do, however, is convince myself each morning that even though I may feel tired, I'm not *actually* tired. I'm fully rested and ready for the ride. I went to bed at a responsible time, and, because of that, my body is equipped with the rest it needs to get up and have a productive day. The reason I can do this is that I figured out the secret:

I **I'm only as tired as I think I am.**

When I wake-up, I'm warm and cozy—and who wants to put their feet down on a cold floor in a quiet house when there's the snooze button to be pushed? That is when the self-talk comes into play. I start talking to myself in different terms. First, when my subconscious tells me I'm too tired and need more sleep, I have an internal conversation and say, sometimes aloud and sometimes in my mind, "Nope, I'm not tired."

Next, I remind myself how great I'm going to feel once I'm up. The hardest part of getting out of bed for me (and for many other people, I imagine) is that initial act of actually rising up out from under the warm covers and into the cold, cruel world. No matter how much sleep you get, there are always a few moments between being fully asleep and fully aware that cause you to second guess whether you're just groggy or may actually need more shuteye.

The third conversation I have with myself is about the alternative. I remind myself that I'm going to be unhappy if I don't get up. The pain of getting up then becomes less than the pain of regretting *not* getting up. I know this because I've experienced it. On those mornings in the past when I slept in, I had this nagging feeling of being behind all day long when I finally got up.

That's the gist of the conversation I have with myself when my alarm buzzes. On most days, this step represents no more than a few seconds or maybe up to a minute. Any more than that, and you may fall asleep again. Don't let the snooze button rob you of your success.

5:40 a.m.
Get in the Zone

After I make my way to my office, I start my favorite part of my morning routine (besides playing with my daughters), which is my meditation time.

Any time I hear about something new, I fight my initial inclination to dismiss it. Most people struggle with new things, and I admit I'm one of them. But there is a beautiful vulnerability that comes with remaining open to things that don't make sense to you.

When I first heard about transcendental meditation, I didn't understand how or why it could work. I was skeptical, but, at the same time, I was also intrigued by the different results it was said to bring. I read a few resources on it but then decided to take the plunge and do a full course to learn how to meditate in an impactful way. Because of that course, I can say that the twenty minutes I spend every morning in meditation are transformative and life-changing.

I don't have a privileged or unique background. I have simply made decisions to rise to the occasion given my circumstances, just like everyone else has the opportunity to do. Meditation allows me to step outside myself and my own ego and clear my thoughts.

> **It allows me to start my day, not on a selfish note, but on one of openness and vulnerability.**

Not everyone has the desire to meditate. If you are spiritual, prayer can provide similar results. My wife has never been into meditation, but she prays every morning. However, I will say that she absolutely loves the effects meditation has brought into my life and therefore encourages me to continue.

This book is not meant to be an instruction on how to meditate, so I will let you research that yourself and find the type of prayer or meditation that works best for you. The type or style matters less than your commitment to just do it.

6 a.m.
Sip and Map

After I finish my meditation, I look forward to having my coffee. I recently removed all added sugar from my diet, and the hardest part of going sugar-free was the thought of going without my decadent dollop of whipped cream on my coffee every morning. *If you haven't tried whipped cream in your coffee, you need to.* Without the whipped cream, life is just not as fun. Fortunately, I discovered sugar-free whipped cream, so now my morning routine is complete once again.

After I make my coffee, I settle in for some mindset and accountability mapping. My meditation time prepares me to answer nine key questions. Before you ask, yes—I answer these same questions every single morning of my life, 365 days a year.

And I recommend you do the same.

You can also find these questions at the end of the book. So, feel free to copy the pages at the end or create your own template to answer questions like this that inspire you, help you focus on your why, and get you in the right mindset as you begin your day.

1. What did I do yesterday to get 1 percent better?

What actions did I take yesterday to improve by even a small percentage? Did I read something that really stayed with me and affected the way I interacted with someone? Was there a training video that helped me become more productive? A huge part of my morning is evaluating my previous day.

2. Who are three people I am grateful for, and did I tell them?

It's one thing to write "I'm grateful for this person." But did I tell them I'm grateful for them and why? If you are interested in growing more meaningful relationships, don't just think about being grateful. Put it out there!

3. What is one thing I am grateful for?

This one thing could be your family, your health, or your mind. There is no limit to what it could be. Take a moment and feel that gratitude.

4. What two goals am I going to schedule and work on today?

What two actions am I going to take today that move me closer to one or more of my quarterly goals? (You'll find more on quarterly goals in the next chapter.) Show your commitment to these things by actually putting them in your calendar.

5. What goals did I accomplish yesterday?

I committed to at least two things yesterday and put them on my calendar. So, it's time to answer the big question: Did I accomplish them?

6. What is one thing that made me smile yesterday?

I love to intentionally find joy in life. When it comes to smiling, nothing makes me smile more than my girls. So, I take it a step further and write down a memory that made me smile. It could be a small moment—just write it down and you'll find yourself smiling once again. That is the kind of energy you want to bring into the next day.

7. What is one new thing I learned yesterday?

This question gets me thinking about what I took from the previous day and how I can continue to apply it to the present moment. If you can't think of something from the day before that you learned, you've got to change that.

8. What is one thing that could have made yesterday better?

What's one thing that I could have done that would have made yesterday even better it was? Even great days can be better. Sometimes, the day gets away from you. This question reminds me to slow down and seek joy in small moments.

9. What did I give yesterday?

Besides myself, who or what did I give to? It could be to your spouse, your kids, or a homeless person. Do small things every day that make big differences in the lives of others. My hairdresser makes house calls, and one day during the pandemic, I tipped him $100. Did the money change his life? Probably not. But I can almost guarantee that it made him feel appreciated (which was my goal). I always look for ways to give because it empowers and encourages others.

I use an app to write all of this down on my iPad. Just be careful when it comes to electronics. I have a rule not to look at my phone before 8 a.m. If you read an email or see a negative social media post, it can completely derail your mindset.

I don't care if it's vibrating, and I don't care if people call me. People who know me know that if it's an emergency before 8 a.m., call 911 because I'm not an ambulance, I'm not a police officer, and I'm not the fire department. My time is my time, and my schedule is under my control.

6:15 a.m.
Read

I give myself up to an hour to read every morning. That translates into about forty-five pages a day. Sometimes, I mix things up and read fifteen pages from three different books. Two of them may be business books, and another an autobiography or biography. I choose not to read fiction. If I do read a fiction book, it is in the evening during my wind-down time. However, most of the time, if I'm going to indulge in some fiction, I'll watch a TV show or a movie instead.

I'm always taking notes. If I hear something in a podcast while working out or while driving that inspires me, I'll stop and make a voice memo to implement it into my day. I call my car my university on wheels, and I love to listen to podcasts while driving.

Whenever I can fill my brain with something that could make me better in some way, I'm all in. I even enjoy reading the same book twice and discovering completely different takeaways once I look back at my notes from each time.

It all depends on where you are in life and what struggles you're dealing with at the moment. Maybe there's a global pandemic, perhaps your wife is pregnant, maybe your career is rocky, or perhaps you are recovering from an accident. Those life experiences will color what you extract from your reading, and your notes will reflect that.

I constantly search for takeaways to implement. The unique thing about reading is it makes you feel like you're having a one-on-one conversation with the author. It's just you and the author, alone at a table, discussing some great ideas and suggestions. If the author happens to point something out to you that you might be doing or not doing, you're more apt to feel convicted about it and pledge to make a change.

> **There's no ego involved when you are reading something and processing it in the privacy of your own mind.**

It's hard to get people to read every day. So, take the pressure off yourself if you're new to it and make small page goals that grow over time. I tell my team to read at least fifteen pages a day, five days a week. This should take around twenty minutes, and if you're a super slow reader, approximately thirty minutes. This is an attainable goal for most readers.

Think about it … suddenly, you've read seventy-five pages in a week and 300 pages in a month!

Reading is essential enough for you to find the time, whether in the morning or the evening.

7:15 a.m.
Move It

My daily workout is an hour. Every other day, I ride my Peloton, and every other day I walk 2.5 miles. I also work out with weights five days a week. If I'm being honest with myself, I don't love working out.

> **But I do love the result, and I know how important it is to my energy levels and overall health to stay active.**

So, I make the time.

During the hour, I listen to podcasts. I used to blast tunes, but now I see the hour as a time to learn from other people. I listen to podcasts instead of audiobooks because it's easier for me to listen to a conversation while working out rather than concentrating on a book.

Some people can digest audiobooks. I found that I was rewinding during my workouts because I missed important points. I choose business and real estate podcasts over any others that are more "entertainment" in nature. An hour is a long time, and I'm not going to waste it.

8:15 a.m.
Schedule Everything

Speaking of a schedule, after I've meditated, mapped, read, and worked out, my calendar is the last massive piece of the puzzle and the one element that ties everything else together.

I schedule every single thing in my day on my calendar. From taking my vitamins to my daily meditation time, I write it all down. Then I look at my calendar and manage it twice a day. I manage it in the morning because my calendar could change based on what goal I have that day or what I've learned. And at the end of the workday, I organize my next day.

Scheduling gives all my meetings a hard stop. I always have another appointment on my calendar. This is key because integrity is critically important to me. I don't lie, so I can't say, "I have to go because I have another appointment on my calendar," unless that is actually true.

Weekends are scheduled, too. I get up and do my morning routine on Saturdays and Sundays because taking a two-day break in the middle of a successful system is a real momentum killer for me. I shift my wake time later by an hour or so, but the steps are still the same.

8:30 a.m.
Create Memories

After I've confirmed my calendar and made adjustments to my schedule, I get ready for the day. I take a quick shower to make sure I have enough time to spend with my daughters before I begin work. This is a brief but critical part of my day.

I intentionally do my calendar as the last step before spending time with my family because I don't want to be wondering what's happening next and whether I have time to be watching a scene from *Frozen* with my girls.

I want to be fully present when I'm with my wife and daughters because I have learned that just fifteen minutes when I'm "all in" is much better than an hour of distracted time. I don't want to be thinking or wondering about what's on tap for the day because I wouldn't be present for my family.

3:30 p.m.
Do a Midday Reset

As you can probably guess, from 9 a.m. until the end of the day, I'm busy. I am managing a multi-state, multi-faceted business with many moving parts, and it's not for the faint of heart.

Even with my pace, there is something I do midday that I highly recommend. I stop and meditate once again for twenty minutes (prayer or even a nap works here, too). The critical takeaway is to stop the madness for a few moments and find some quiet solitude to refocus on what is important and remember that goal you set for the day, as well as the things for which you are grateful.

During the pandemic, my afternoon meditation helped keep me grounded and rational when so much stress, fear, and worry had been coming at me through conversations and reports from the media.

You may need to adjust this meditation time depending on when you start and stop your workday. For me, 3:30 p.m. works because I work until 7 p.m. I also know that after my afternoon reset, I'm going to get eight hours of work done in three hours because I'm laser focused.

My afternoon meditation looks virtually the same as my morning session, and it doesn't even matter if I'm not home or at the office.

Wherever I am, I stop and unplug for twenty minutes. I turn off the light, if possible, and put in my noise-canceling Air Pods.

7 p.m.
Get Home and Chill

At the end of my day, I'm ready to unwind and see my family's smiling faces. I leave my office by 7 p.m., and I'm home by 7:30 p.m.

I work with my oldest daughter Luna on her school skills. My wife teaches the kids Spanish, so I come home and teach them English. Then I give baths and do bedtime every night. My wife jokes that my girls will be sixteen years old, and I'm still going to be rocking them to sleep. And she may just be right because it's something I wouldn't trade for the world.

I also don't look at my phone after 7:30 p.m. because that is my family's time. I also don't want to put useless nonsense in my head before I go to sleep.

At night, any nonfiction books I read are generally more spiritual or inspirational in nature. I really enjoy books like *The Greatness Guide* and *The Greatest Salesman in the World*. I'll read anything that is thought-provoking about life and what motivates us.

The evening is also a great time to read rather than turn on the TV. I prefer not to watch TV and fill my head with images of violence or fear. Everyone is different, but I don't like it for a few reasons—one of which is that the blue light adversely affects my sleep, and sleep is the single most important thing I do every single day.

SUCCESS IS A SNOWFLAKE

I've been adhering to this schedule for four-plus years. Now, I had great success in business before I started doing this every day. So, what changed? I've run a lucrative business compared to most people, but what I realized is I need to stop comparing myself to "most people" and set a new bar.

We get caught up in comparisons, and this has been made significantly worse by social media. We look at someone else's success and compare it to ours. Or maybe we look at friends and think, *I'm doing better than them, so I'm good.* If that is the case, you probably need some new friends.

If you aren't being pushed by your circle, you need a new circle.

There are no two people on this planet who have the same level of success. So, the question is not, *What can I do to catch up to other people?* The question is, *What can I do to take my life to the next level on* my *terms?*

> **Success is like a snowflake. Yours and someone else's will never look exactly the same.**

I want to reiterate that success is not just monetary or business-related, and I'll never be able to say that enough. It's personal; it's family; it's friendships; it's the stuff of life.

Unfortunately, modern society has taught us that we cannot be satisfied until we reach some finite point of success. This has also become the curse of social media because we're never happy with our lives when we see others' perceived success online.

Everyone else seems to be so *#blessed*, right?

So, is there really ever true happiness? I believe there is, and it exists at every single level of success. But don't confuse *happiness* for *contentment*. You should always want to fight to get to the next level. There may come a time when you become satisfied and accept where you are. If you're happy with that, great! If you're not satisfied with that, then that tells you everything you need to know—and you have not yet reached your *own* definition of success.

I can always be a better husband, a better father, a better employer, a better businessman, and a better mentor to people. I have set those expectations for myself and move heaven and earth to achieve them.

There are actually only two categories of people for which you can have expectations. The first is the people you pay. Money is a contract for a good or service. If I'm buying a $50 filet in a restaurant, I expect that filet to look and taste a certain way and for the service to be exemplary. I have a right to expect that. I can go to Whole Foods and buy a filet for $20, but I'm willing to pay more to be served and treated well.

Your family, including your spouse, does not fit into that first category. The only expectations I can have of my wife are the vows we shared. I cannot expect her to cook me dinner every single day, be in a great mood all the time, or give me a ten-second kiss before I leave for work.

If you set unrealistic expectations of others, the "100-Percent Rule" will apply, and that is: *You are going to be let down 100 percent of the time.*

Your partner, kids, family, and friends all have such vastly diverse life experiences, thanks to the differences in our thought processes. We each have thousands of subconscious thoughts that color the lens through which we view life.

Our subconscious mind or inner thought life is a part of the problem when it comes to expectations. When someone does not fulfill expectations that you have unfairly set for them, you give that "failure" meaning. Maybe your spouse isn't as affectionate lately because she's stressed. Your brain gives the lack of attention undue importance, and you start to think, *She doesn't love me as much as she used to.*

The reality is that lack of affection has nothing to do with you. Zero. But you give it meaning and then create this story in your subconscious that keeps it going in a vicious cycle. Sadly, those are the kinds of seeds that can destroy relationships.

The only other person for which you can set expectations is yourself. That also means if you're going to make promises or set expectations for yourself, you'd better keep them. But guess what? Very few people do. We break promises to ourselves multiple times a day. Just imagine for a second if you got as mad at yourself as you get at other people for letting you down.

The reason we can let ourselves off the hook so quickly is that we don't tell anybody the "deals" we make with ourselves that we break. You have to tell other people what you are doing or plan to do. This is the essence of *accountability*, and it's an indispensable part of this process.

SUCCESS REQUIRES ACCOUNTABILITY

I'm not a superhero, nor do I have any inherent talents that make me more prone to adhering to a schedule than others. I like to learn, and I want to keep doing what works and scrapping what doesn't.

I've always had a good work ethic, but my routine used to bring more harm than health into my body. When I started with Allstate after switching from New York Life, it took every dime (and then some) I had to start my first agency. I hired my first employee six months in and used a credit card to pay her. That's how broke I was.

Somehow, I convinced myself that the shower at the gym was sufficient. I worked ninety to 100 hours a week and didn't see the point in paying rent for some tiny apartment where I'd never be. So, I lived in my car for three months. It was the definition of *grind*. Let's just say it was a good thing I was single at the time because there is no way that a person can have a meaningful home life (or any kind of life) with the schedule I had.

I eventually realized that you don't have to kill yourself to be successful. I would get up at 7 a.m. or even 8 a.m. and work until late at night and was still growing a large, multi-state business.

Years down the road, I finally got married and had a child. Suddenly, I realized that if I wanted a successful business *and* a successful home life, it was time to start getting up earlier to make improvements that would make me a better husband, father, and coach.

Without a system for the morning in place, you wake up and *BAM!* Life hits you, and you are forced to hit the ground running.

Once the rest of the world up with you, there is too much of a risk for interruptions.

> **Get up in the quiet stillness of the morning, and you will notice a dramatic shift in every part of your life.**

I knew I needed to make the commitment, and, when I finally did, I told everyone around me what my new plan was—my wife, my friends, and even my employees. I wanted them all to hold me accountable.

I even inspired other people to start the routine with me. We would text each other every morning to make sure we were up. It was incredible and made getting up more doable, knowing that I'd soon be getting a call or needing to make that call myself.

A few years ago, I set another rule that the cell phone would go away at 7:30 p.m. and not come back out until 8 a.m. the next day. Then I told my wife about the plan and asked her to hold me accountable. If I had made this rule but not involved her, I could more easily break it. It could also cause resentment if she brought up my phone use without me first bringing her on board as an accountability partner.

When you ask someone to hold you accountable, and then you slip, and that person calls you out, your ego gets involved, and that's a good thing (more on ego later). I hate the thought of trying to explain to someone why something didn't get done or that I broke a promise. Some people don't care, but most people do. I hope you're one of those people.

If you currently go to bed with the best of intentions but then hit snooze in the morning, what can you do? First, you have to commit to yourself, and then you have to tell other people about it.

If you don't tell anyone, the odds are it will never happen. It will continue being an unfulfilled intention—a daydream. The most crucial step is to tell everyone, especially the people closest to you, to hold you accountable.

Accountability outside of ourselves is useful because we live in a self-centered world. We all are egomaniacs. People can say they're not, but every one of us is egocentric. Think about this—if you take a group picture, who is the first person you're going to look at in that photo? We're all egotistical to a degree and worry about what other people think of us.

If you think you aren't an egomaniac, then you're an even bigger one.

This means that the best way to foster a Success Psyche is to make sure you're telling people what you plan to do and give them permission to hold you to it. Tell them your morning routine goals, weight loss goals, business goals, social media limits, whatever it may be. Then empower those people to call you out and help you get back on track.

> If your commitment is going to stick, it's got to move from being *subconscious and internal* to *conscious and external*.

Get it out of your head and into the world. If you aren't prepared to do that, you aren't prepared to make any real changes. You're just trying to make yourself feel better in the short term.

If you need to start working out, create a workout group that you meet every morning at 6 a.m. Chances are slim you're going to leave those people waiting outside without you. I started a book club for accountability, and we meet every Wednesday to discuss the book of the month. I could not imagine letting those people down. It is just not who I am.

Getting the big results requires doing the hard things. For me, the way to get through those moments when you want to hit the snooze (literally and figuratively in life) is to just lean into it. When you don't feel like getting up, that's when you do it. It's a brain switch, and success requires you to flip that switch.

I know that many people hesitate to embark on something like an early morning routine because they've heard you've got to do the hard work now for the big payoff way on down the road. They know they need to do the tough things for the long-term gains.

But the truth is, the results are far more instantaneous. When I get up and don't hit the snooze button, I instantly feel better. I feel proud of myself and know how many things I'm going to get accomplished. I get an instant reward from that.

Habits are built because of rewards.

It really does *not* have to be only for long-term gain. You can enjoy rewards immediately. You aren't just getting up early to gain some bonus over the long term (well, you are), but you *also* can enjoy instant gratification.

BABY STEPS ARE STILL STEPS

I'm an all-in kind of guy. When I started with the elements of my morning plan, I did them with full force. That's just how I'm wired.

But it's not the only way to make it happen.

For the people who aren't all-in, you still have to commit, but the commitment can be to do hard things in small bites. Little moves still put you in the right direction. As long as you have a why you can find a way to do something. One of the things I always say is this:

> **Change your way, change your life.**

Make a decision that you're going to do it no matter how painful it is.

- Wake up and meditate for five minutes.
- Mindset map and goal set for three minutes.
- Read for five minutes.
- Go for a short quarter-mile walk.

Then just keep taking those same steps repeatedly and slowly increase the time invested in each step over time.

And don't forget the all-important step to set expectations. Make a promise to yourself and tell people.

A lot of people complain about their lives. They complain about the way they were raised. Complaining is a waste. We have no control over what country we were born in or what family we were born into or whether or not we had enough to eat as kids.

You have to change your ways to change your life. A solid morning routine will, without a doubt, change your life if you stick to it, even in smaller increments.

Do your habits serve you, or are you a slave to your habits?

The word *habit* has a completely different meaning, depending entirely on how disciplined you are. If you already have a routine and are disciplined, then you view the word *habit* in a positive light. If you struggle to wake up early, get distracted by social media during the day, feel regretful at the end of a workday at how little you accomplished, and go to bed by the glow of TV, then I imagine the word *habit* to you is more negative.

Well, here is what I know. If you want to develop a Success Psyche, your habits are going to have to serve you, not the other way around.

Do you train for what you want, every single day? If you are going to be a pro, you need to train like one.

Do you have a system to ensure you are implementing good habits? This book will help you do just that. What about a system to destroy the bad habits? The same routine you develop to incorporate good habits will help you flush out the bad ones.

Read the right books every morning—ones filled with inspiration and sound coaching advice from other successful people, and you'll see which habits you have that need to be replaced.

> **If you get nothing else from this book, understand that what you do first thing in the morning will either create success or frustration throughout the rest of your day.**

Make hard choices. Do the hard things. If you are staying up too late at night watching TV and that's making it impossible for you to get up in the morning, move the TV remote to the other end of the house. I play tricks on myself like this every day to get stuff done.

I have learned how to manipulate my own mind. I would never attempt to control someone else's mind, but my own—I'll manipulate it all day long. This is an essential process because we're always listening to that subconscious record player in our head, the one from childhood that tries to program us to fail.

We all know why we don't act or follow through on a goal. We just don't admit it to anybody around us. We just start excusing ourselves because we're not accountable to anyone else.

I've made lots of mistakes in my life, including failing with how I start my day. I've always done a little bit of reading, but it used to be sporadic. I also never meditated until I started my new schedule. Now that I have made all of these things a part of my daily routine, I cannot imagine ever going back.

I finally figured out what drives the egomaniac in me—and that's not breaking promises to people. I used to think I was some sort of angel because I always prided myself on being "a man of my word." If I told you I would do something, then I would do it, no matter what.

I figured out that I'm no angel.

I'm just an egomaniac who doesn't want to look bad.

It may be hard for you to admit how much ego drives our decisions, but I hope you'll see that it's not something to be embarrassed about by the end of this book. Instead, embrace it and use it to help you find the accountability you need to set up a winning morning process.

IN THE LONG RUN,
MEN HIT ONLY
WHAT THEY
AIM AT.

HENRY DAVID THOREAU

SIX

USE A GPS FOR VISION AND VALUES

Would you believe me if I told you I have a vision board on my fridge, on my bathroom mirror, and as the screensaver on both my iPhone and iPad?

Yes, I'm talking about that clichéd board of photos that was a fad motivation tool in the early 2000s. Across the country, young women enthusiastically cut out pictures of bikini models, and men snipped pictures of Ferraris and washboard abs. For a time, these collages full of visual wonder covered everyone's mirrors and dashboards.

These days, vision boards seem to have faded away (as most fads do). However, the truth is that if they didn't work for you before, it's because you were using them wrong.

Goal mapping with a visual board is incredible. That is why I plan to bring them back and make vision boards awesome again.

I also plan to completely change the way you look at goal setting/planning and make it possible to set and consistently achieve your goals.

No matter what type of learner you think you are (sight, hearing, or touch), the truth is that *all* human beings are visual. Our eyes take in data, and our brains process that visual stimuli, which makes life exciting, fresh, and tangible.

I know some people love to watch a musician sit on a stool and play guitar for two hours, but let's be real. Most people go to a concert to see a big show—an impressive production that's a treat to the senses. If we just wanted to listen to music, we've all got Spotify or Apple Music on our phones.

We don't need to pay $150 a ticket to *listen* to the show. We go to *see* the show.

We make memories with our eyes, and those visual memories get locked away, and we never forget them. The power of visuals is a fundamental reason behind why goal mapping through vision boards is so useful.

And I'm talking about more than just a board with words on it. You need the pictures. You need the eye candy.

I will also say that not all vision boards are created equally. I've seen vision boards that make my head spin with its random pictures all over the place. It makes me dizzy just thinking about it. Those types of vision boards are useless.

Honestly, just throw those in the trash.

The only way to create a vision board that works is through careful planning and execution (just like everything else in life worth having and using). I'm talking about a vision board that is the tangible, visual version of your most important goals.

THE HOW-TO OF A KILLER GOALS COLLAGE

The best vision boards are clean and visually streamlined. If someone else looks at your vision board and can't tell what's going on, that is not a good vision board. It should be evident to anyone who even remotely knows you what each visual represents.

I don't bother listing a wordy, detailed description of each goal represented on the board. I already write down my goals every morning during my mindset mapping time, so I don't need them spelled out word for word on my vision board.

How to create a visually clean collage:

I found a phenomenal online resource that helps you create a vision board easily and for free: *www.PhotoCollage.com*. It's the simplest process and takes less than five minutes to create your own board. Just go to the website and drop in your pictures or images—that's it!

The benefit of creating your board on *www.PhotoCollage.com* is that you now have a digital copy of it saved on your computer and phone, as well as one you can print.

To maximize the advantages, use your vision board as the screensaver on your devices. Then, print it off and put it on the bathroom mirror. Most of us look at ourselves first thing in the morning, so you can add your board to the list of things you see when you get up. Daily reminders can only help, never hurt.

I love resources that make my life simpler, and *www.PhotoCollage.com* is one of those resources. It's so crucial for me to make the process easy because I create a new board every ninety days, bringing us to the next point.

How to set a time frame that gets results:

Don't create a vision board that quickly becomes a nebulous picture on the wall. To be effective, your board must be a precise representation of your goals. That's why I create a new board every ninety days.

That also means I create a new set of goals every ninety days (we'll discuss more on this later in the chapter).

I choose goals that will bring me closer to my unique success definition. If an action does not bring me closer to that definition, I don't bother with it.

I know a lot of people who create long-term (one- to five-year) vision boards. A year is too long, and anything longer than that is useless. Those things end up in the trash or collecting dust where no one looks at them.

Suppose you say to yourself, *By the end of the year, I want to accomplish this goal.* The tendency most have to procrastinate means that all you'll end up with is some unfulfilled dreams that make you feel regretful at the end of the year.

So, every ninety days, I sit down and create new goals. If there is an important goal that I did not reach in the previous ninety days, it rolls over into the next ninety days. If this happens more than two times in a row, I evaluate whether that is a goal I desire or need to achieve.

How to cover both personal and family goals:

My personal vision board hangs on the fridge. My family has a communal vision board as well. One of the most bonding activities you can do as a family is to sit down and create a vision board together.

Each family member gets at least one goal directly related to them on the vision board. My young daughters have no way of choosing their own goals yet, so my wife and I set goals related to them, such as daily learning time and Spanish/English practice. My teenage son typically has a school or a sports goal, and we set the expectation that he will report back to us on his progress weekly.

Teach your kids this skill because school doesn't cover this real-life kind of stuff (it's sad but true).

Our family vision board is also meant to last ninety days. We sit down once a week and discuss whether we are on track to meet our goals. We call it a family meeting, and it's a time of encouragement and accountability.

If we don't accomplish a goal, we put a red X through it as a strong visual. It's important to let your kids know that failure is always a valuable lesson and not something to never speak of again.

After my son and I watched the Michael Jordan documentary *The Last Dance* together, he felt inspired to start practicing basketball more. The next day, he went outside for fifteen minutes but then came back in to check his cell phone. I noticed this and remarked, "One of the reasons Michael Jordan was so successful was he didn't have the distraction of a cell phone."

My son looked up from his phone, and I could tell this convicted him (you never know with teenagers, but at that moment, the accountability resonated with him).

"You're not wrong," he replied.

The only reason I was able to say this to him is that we've given each other permission to hold each other accountable. You don't want any resentment when you remind your family members to keep working on their goals. So, when you communicate your intentions from the start, it has the potential to be more well-received.

If your family has trouble spending time together, make it a goal to have family dinners at least three times a week. Make it a goal to have a family game night once a week or to get outside and play sports together. I know it sounds strange to *plan* to make memories, but with the pace of life, do what you can to make sure you love the people who need it most.

My business vision board is the one that I keep on my bathroom mirror and my devices' screen savers. I also expect my employees to do their own vision boards. From their first day working within my organization, I ask them what they would like to accomplish over the next ninety days. They should determine what successes will be essential within their first three months, based on what they learned during training.

How to use it daily:

Reviewing my vision board is a part of my weekly routine. Every Monday at 4 p.m., I have an appointment to see how well I am progressing in each vision board goal and what adjustments may be necessary.

Am I off track? What actions do I need to take over the next few days or weeks to get back on track?

A vision board is not a substitute for a detailed plan, and the mere act of creating one will not make you successful. However, reviewing your board does help you plan your days with precision and efficiency.

> **Your vision board represents the destinations you are trying to reach, and your goals are a part of the GPS that gets you there.**

A vision board is only as good as the goals that helped to make it. This chapter is, at its very core, a detailed explanation of my unique goal-setting process and how you can quickly adapt it and use it in your own life.

So, let's talk about the process of goal setting and how to use your vision board as a launching pad for creating what I refer to as a winning **GPS**, short for *Goal Planning System*.

IMPLEMENTING YOUR CUSTOM GPS

I never leave my house without using my favorite GPS (global positioning system) app called Waze.

It's the best way to get me from point A to B most efficiently and via the fastest route. I wouldn't even think of navigating a trip to anywhere further than the neighborhood market without my **GPS** programming ready to guide me. It can maneuver me around accidents and save me so much time and frustration.

Yet, people leave their proverbial doorstep every day with no GPS in hand—and it really shows. They have no end goals in mind and no plan to get to where they need to go. My favorite question to ask people is this:

> *If I gave you a magic wand, how much money would you like to make every month that would enable you to live the life of your dreams?*

Few people can answer this question. Even fewer have an answer ready to go on the tip of their tongues. So, let's stop for a minute to think about that question and come up with an answer.

This lack of direction and guidance also shows when I ask them about their business or work goals. I might ask, "How many marketing partners do you want to bring into business this month?"

The responses usually sound like, "I guess I'd like to bring in five."

Oh, you'd "like" to? So, is that your goal? And how are you going to reach that goal? What activity does that represent?

Without a **GPS** to direct you, that number is really just a wish. So, let's talk about how to fix that. There are three straightforward steps to reach your goal according to my *Goal Planning System,* or **GPS**.

1. Pick a Few Carefully Selected Destinations.

First things first, people set way too many goals at a time. How many burners are on most stoves? Four. That's the same number of goals that happen to work for me. I have found the sweet spot seems to be somewhere between four to seven goals for most people.

I memorize my goals so that I can easily rewrite them at the top of the page during my mindset mapping and scheduling each morning. Then, I base that day's specific goals upon these larger quarterly goals. I design each day's particular tasks to move the ball forward on one of my primary vision board goals.

Overdoing it on goals can be highly demotivating and cause you to stop the process altogether. Start with four goals and increase from there only once you complete all four for the quarter. Goal setting is not an exact process, and every person needs to tweak and make personalized settings and adjustments.

Four seems to be the magic number in my life for another reason as well. Anyone who knows me knows that I love sports. I'm a massive fan of football and basketball and its application to every area of life because I see a football game as a business—and I run my business like a football game.

When you're watching a football game, there are two things you follow closely the entire time: You're following the *score*, and you're watching the *clock*. I mimic this every single day in my business.

If it's the second quarter and I'm already far ahead, I don't take my foot off the gas because I know even great teams lose championships this way. You never take your eye off the ball. By the same logic, if you're going into the fourth quarter and losing by three touchdowns, there is still time to make a comeback.

There's always time for a comeback until the final seconds are gone.

This gamified way of approaching my day also means that not every single game is a win. That's okay. If you can't tell by now, I relish failure because it shows me what doesn't work and almost always reveals a path to what *does* work.

Football is a game of yards. You don't use Hail Mary touchdown passes every time you score. The consistently superior teams work on their ground game, one yard at a time, to get to the end zone.

2. Plan the Routes You Will Take Every Day.

A vision board like the one we discussed leads naturally into the reverse engineering process that transforms goals into more than pipe dreams.

If a baseball player wants a batting average of .350, how many hours a day does he need to practice? What questions does he need to ask his coach? What exercises should he be doing every day or every week?

If a salesperson wants to hit a certain quota, what sales numbers will it take? How many customers does that represent, and how much does each customer have to be worth? What is that salesperson's closing percentage—and so how many prospects does that mean he needs to be calling to close enough customers? These are the kinds of questions you must reverse engineer before you plan a single moment of another day.

These questions enable you to discover what Goal Producing Activities, or *GPAs*, are going to get you to your goals.

Still, goals are a source of pain and struggle for so many people. How many times have you set a goal in your mind or even gone so far as to write it down, and then a few months or a year later, you realize you fell short of achieving it?

It's a terrible feeling. It's a sinking feeling. It's also a feeling that you don't have to experience anymore. From now on, you are going to divide your day into quarters, and you will use your **GPS** planning sheet to determine what **GPAs** you will do every quarter.

I have developed and utilized a patented spreadsheet system that I call the **Four Quarters GPS**. Remember, **GPS** stands for my *Goal Planning System*. The **Four Quarters GPS** is a simple and effective goal planning spreadsheet that you can use in literally any business. It can transform any career—from sales, insurance, and mortgage brokers to real estate, car sales, network marketing, and beyond. On the following page is a representation of the spreadsheet I've developed. If you would like to download the Excel version for free, visit my website at: *www.TheSuccessPsyche.com/GPS*.

Here is the most efficient way to break down your goals and plan your **GPAs**:

Yearly Quarters

First, I set four to seven (typically closer to four) goals per quarter. That also means I have four goal setting sessions per year. I revisit these goals every day throughout each quarter:

FOUR QUARTERS GPS

Goal · Planning · System

DATE/QTR	MP'S GOAL	MP'S ACTUAL	VIP'S GOAL	VIP'S ACTUAL	BLOCKS GOAL	BLOCK'S ACTUAL	RANK GOAL	RANK ACTUAL	INCOME GOAL	INCOME ACTUAL
Q____ Yr.____										
Month____										
Week #1										
Week #2										
Week #3										
Week #4										
Daily (M-Th)										
Month____										
Week #1										
Week #2										
Week #3										
Week #4										
Daily (M-Th)										
Month____										
Week #1										
Week #2										
Week #3										
Week #4										
Daily (M-Th)										

FOUR QUARTERS GPS

Goal · Planning · System

GPA (Goal Producing Activity)

80% of your time

GOAL AREA	DATE/QTR	GOAL	ACTUAL	GOAL	ACTUAL	GOAL	ACTUAL
	Month ___						
	Each Week						
	Daily (M–Th)						
	Each Quarter of the Day						

GOAL AREA	DATE/QTR	GOAL	ACTUAL	GOAL	ACTUAL	GOAL	ACTUAL
	Month ___						
	Each Week						
	Daily (M–Th)						
	Each Quarter of the Day						

GOAL AREA	DATE/QTR	GOAL	ACTUAL	GOAL	ACTUAL	GOAL	ACTUAL
	Month ___						
	Each Week						
	Daily (M–Th)						
	Each Quarter of the Day						

20% of your time

GOAL AREA	DATE/QTR	GOAL	ACTUAL	GOAL	ACTUAL	GOAL	ACTUAL
	Month ___						
	Each Week						
	Daily (M–Th)						
	Each Quarter of the Day						

Quarter 1: January through March
Quarter 2: April through June
Quarter 3: July through September
Quarter 4: October through December

Monthly Quarters

Next, I look at each week of the month as a quarter. My goal is to achieve what I have set out to do for that month within the first four weeks. I consider any time beyond day twenty-eight to be overtime that I can use to catch up and ensure a victory:

Quarter 1: Week 1
Quarter 2: Week 2
Quarter 3: Week 3
Quarter 4: Week 4
Overtime: Days 29+

Weekly Quarters

Third, I look at my work week in the same manner, in that Monday through Thursday are quarters one through four. My goal is to accomplish everything I need to achieve for the week by Thursday. Friday is my overtime day and the time that I use to catch up and again ensure a victory:

Quarter 1: Monday
Quarter 2: Tuesday
Quarter 3: Wednesday
Quarter 4: Thursday
Overtime: Friday

Daily Quarters

Finally, I separate each day into quarters. At the end of every quarter, I come to the sidelines for some "huddle time" to discuss the next few plays, so the day doesn't get away from me.

Quarter 1: 9 to 11 a.m.
Quarter 2: 11 a.m. to 1 p.m.
Quarter 3: 1 to 3 p.m.
Quarter 4: 3 to 5 p.m.
Overtime: Beyond 5 p.m.

So, now to the really good stuff. How can you use this information to construct a plan for each quarter, each month, each week, and each day to achieve your goals? I'll explain how to do this with a simple example:

Let's say you are in sales, and you've determined your average commission per customer is $1,000. One of your goals is to make $60,000 for the quarter ($20,000 a month) in commission. That also means your goal for the quarter is to gain 60 new customers for the quarter (20 customers a month).

How do you take that information and put the numbers into your **GPS** in order to plan your **GPA**?

First, you need your closing ratio:

What is the average number of people you talk to who say yes? (If you've never figured this out, you need to.) Take the number of reaches or calls you make in a month and divide that by the number of people who become customers.

For this example, let's assume your closing ratio is 10 percent. Since you want to close 60 customers that quarter, how many people will you need to talk to?

Well, 60 is 10 percent of 600. So, that's 600 calls for the quarter, which may sound like a lot. But it doesn't seem so daunting when you start to break it down (and this is where the magic happens).

600 calls / 3 months = 200 calls per month.
200 calls / 4 weeks = 50 calls a week.
50 call / 4 days (remember, Friday is overtime) =
    13 calls a day (round up)
13 calls / 4 quarters in a day = 4 calls per daily quarter

So, in order to reach a goal that seemed so massive at a 30,000-foot view, all you need to do is have *four conversations every two hours of the day*. That's literally just two calls every hour, and you'll be making $20,000 a month in commissions. Can you call two people in an hour?

Sure you can.

3. Start Driving and Make Sure You Stay on the Route.

Once you've determined the activity needed, the last step is to schedule that activity on your calendar. Don't just assume you'll do it now that you've figured it out. Write it down and leave nothing to chance.

Make the commitment by putting it into your calendar. If it doesn't get scheduled, it doesn't get done.

Because I've broken my goals down to the smallest daily quarters, I know exactly how much activity I will need to do each day to achieve my quarterly goals.

In addition to my **GPS** spreadsheet, I also keep a checklist of essential pieces to my **GPS** and my **GPAs** that I internalize. Here are the questions I ask myself every week (either on Sunday or Monday):

1. Did I write down my goals?
2. Did I look at them daily? (If you keep score, you'll win.)
3. Have I identified the people I need to help me?
4. Do I have the exact **GPA** to accomplish my goals, and are my **GPAs** the actions that fill my daily calendar?
5. Is my goal attainable in ninety days? If not, what is a more attainable date and what is the fastest route to get there?
6. What benefits will I and those around me gain from reaching my goal?
7. What skill/knowledge do I need to get there?
8. Have I truly committed to this goal by telling everyone around me?
9. Can I visualize this goal being attained?
10. Will reaching this goal bring me happiness?
11. Have I identified potential obstacles?
12. What are the consequences if I don't do what it takes to hit my goals?

Clarity precedes success, and awareness precedes transformation. These questions will provide you with the clarity needed that leads to eventual transformation. No matter how many goals you set and how determined you think you are, you will fail if you:

- Do not believe you can achieve it.
- Do not execute through daily **GPA**.
- Do not remind yourself daily of the promises and commitments you have made.

Do you see how doable a **GPS** and the **GPAs** make the process? The **GPS** provides you with all the pieces you need to turn pipe dreams into workable destinations with four steps:

1. Determine the goal.
2. Determine the activity.
3. Schedule the activity.
4. Make the daily commitment.

I like to live life as a game. It's more effective, and it also has the distinct advantage of being more fun. Start viewing life as something worth training for and playing hard. The other alternative is to let the current of life sweep you along with it.

We should all work to become studiers of our craft. It could be in sales, teaching, or corporate America. We can all become elite professionals in whatever we do.

"But, Jay, what if I miss a goal?"

Sometimes, life happens, and goals don't get met. After all, the only thing sure in life is that everything changes. You may have a daughter who used to get up at 8:30 a.m. who now gets up at 7 a.m. (I know a thing or two about this). Such a shift could change the way your morning looks. You may have started a new side hustle since the last time you set your ninety-day goals.

There will be setbacks, and you may have losing seasons. Sports teams suffer from poor leadership, injuries, or a new competitive team. Your business may lose employees or face a hotshot competitor.

Don't forget this essential piece: When the day (game) is over, you have to review the film. That is what you do every morning during mindset mapping and calendar time. You can't leave the office today, come back tomorrow, do the same plays, and expect different results.

What did you do in the first quarter that got you off track? Did you call enough people in the second quarter? Did you get distracted in the third quarter by your phone or a social media post? Did you take your head out of the game too early in the fourth quarter? How honest can you be with yourself about how much time you waste every day?

If you aren't ready to answer these types of questions, then you aren't prepared to develop a Success Psyche.

Dividing my life into quarters and using my **GPS** (and plugging those **GPAs** into it) has revolutionized my workday.

Sure, you will have setbacks, just like any great athlete does. But I prefer to call them *learning experiences*, which then become opportunities to create something greater than intended.

Things happen, so you've got to stay flexible. You've also got to stay committed to your schedule and not allow distractions that are *not* on your calendar to creep in and steal your most precious commodity (time).

If you don't take control, the results could be catastrophic.

Are you engaging in **GPAs** every day?

Is your calendar filled with **GPAs**?

We must all suffer from one of two pains: the pain of discipline or the pain of regret.

> **The pain of discipline is fleeting, but the pain of regret lasts a lifetime.**

Proper use of time through effective time management is another key to developing a success psyche. There are countless books and seminars on the subject—and that's because it's an almost *universal* area of struggle for people.

I would like you to commit to overcoming the tendency to misuse your time.

Here is an example of the pain of wasted time. If you waste twenty minutes an hour in a workday (from being poorly trained, disorganized, distracted, tired, bored, scrolling on social media, etc.), let's see how much time you've really wasted ....

Compound effect of wasting twenty minutes an hour in a typical workday:

- 20 minutes per hour x 40-hour workweek =
  800 minutes a week wasted
- 800 minutes a week x 4 weeks a month =
  3,200 minutes a month wasted
- 3,200 minutes a month / 60 minutes an hour =
  53.33 hours a month wasted
- 53.33 hours per month / 24 hours a day =
  2.22 days a month wasted
- 2.22 days a month x 12 months =
  26.64 days a year wasted

And that's just the time you wasted during a typical length workday. In reality, most of us "work" far more than eight hours. We have families and responsibilities at home. The majority of people have around fourteen hours of daily life. So, let's do one more example, this time showing the result of wasting that same "insignificant" twenty minutes an hour.

Compound effect of wasting twenty minutes an hour in a typical fourteen-hour day:

- 20 minutes per hour x 14-hour day =
  280 minutes a day wasted
- 280 minutes a day x 7 days a week =
  1,960 minutes a week wasted
- 1,960 minutes a week x 52 weeks a year =
  101,920 minutes a year wasted
- 101,920 minutes a year / 60 minutes an hour =
  1,698.67 hours a year wasted
- 1,698.67 hours / 24 hours a day =
  70.78 days a year wasted

More than *two entire months* of your life every year—just *gone* with nothing to show for it. *Talk about the compound effect!* Remember all those times you complained about not having enough time? Yeah, it turns out that is not exactly true, is it?

Schedule your day or live with the pain of regret!

THE SECRET INGREDIENT IS THE RIGHT SET OF VALUES

One of the things I do every quarter is ensure that every goal I create aligns with the core values that guide my business and life.

You can have goals, and you can have pictures on a vision board, but without the core values that guide you, you will be like one of those sad people we hear about from time to time. You know the type—they lived a life of wealth and luxury, but we find out that they were secretly miserable their entire lives.

In case you didn't already realize it, it's possible to be wealthy—and even accomplish goals—but be miserable.

Many different things contribute to the happiness or unhappiness of a person's life. Still, I have noticed that without internalized values to guide you, you will struggle to find joy and remain true to your ethical plumbline.

So, what are core values? Core values are things that you believe in no matter what and no matter when. They are values that allow you to evaluate every situation, every person, and every decision according to a uniform set of guidelines.

Core values make it extremely easy for me to make decisions about my goals and actions. If an activity does not align with my core values, I don't consider it. If a potential new hire seems to contradict one of my core values, I won't hire them. If I have to betray one of my core values to achieve a goal, it's not a goal worth pursuing.

Here are the ten core values that guide my life and business.

1. Exude Excellence

I am passionate about excellence. It's the number one trait I look for in companies that I work with and the employees that I hire. Life is too short to expect or do mediocre work. Anyone that I employ represents me, so they must also strive for excellence. I look for people who are intentional about excellence. I also want employees who will ask for feedback to ensure that they are delivering excellent work.

I don't want to work with anyone ashamed of their excellence. If you are the best at what you do, you deserve praise. Just make sure that if you say you are the best at what you do, you can back up that claim.

2. Have a Positive Attitude

I do my best to operate with a positive attitude every day. I also only surround myself with people who have an intentionally positive attitude. The reason is simple: It's next to impossible to be positive amidst a sea of negativity.

The world comes at us hard every single day. From the news to social media to our past insecurities and failure psyches trying to bring us down, there is a lot stacked against us. Having a positive attitude is the only thing that will get you past the failure and onto the successes.

I ask people to be infectious with their positive attitudes in an effort to dispel the negativity of others. If I walk into an office and see someone frowning, I smile at them. If they don't smile back, I ask them in a joking way if their lips are broken. Such a question almost always puts a smile on their face. You should strive to be the kind of person who puts a smile on other people's faces.

Your world could be crashing down around you, but you'd better make sure your customers and clients don't see that. If you need to go home and cry after work, then do it. Just don't put that type of stress on your work family or your clients. Put on a happy face and spread some cheer. The only other alternative is bringing people down with you, and that's not what winners do.

3. Be a Team Player

At this point in the book, it should be evident that I love sports. I use sports analogies every single day with my employees. So, it shouldn't come as a surprise that everyone I work around absolutely has to be a team player.

You must keep track of what you're doing and allow other people to hold you accountable. You can't be a glory hound, and you absolutely must be able to play well with others. There are no exceptions to this.

You've also got to be humble and unrelentingly kind to everyone around you. Another critical piece of this core value is that you must give more than you expect in return. If you're doing for others with expectations or stipulations attached, you are not a team player.

4. Be Driven

Having a Success Psyche means that you challenge yourself every day. The biggest competitor you will ever face in life is *you* from yesterday. You can always do better than that version of yourself! You shouldn't compare yourself to others. Ultimately, you should compare yourself only to yesterday's performance.

Yes, we can play games and be competitive with others, but ,ultimately, it's how you play against yourself. When you make a mistake, you have to own it. You can't blame the team. Someone with a strong internal drive does this almost intrinsically, and I love to work around people who think this way.

5. Always Evolve

The way you did business five years ago or even one year ago is not the same way you should do business today. The global coronavirus pandemic taught us many things—and one of the most important lessons was this: *Evolve or get left behind.* The companies that shifted their business models rapidly were the ones that thrived during 2020.

When I hear people say something like, "But this is the way we've always done it," I can't run away from them fast enough. I don't care how you used to do it. I want to know how you're going to do it in the future to serve your customers in a way that benefits them, not just you.

If there is a new technology that will benefit your clients and your business, you should have adopted it yesterday. Don't be one of those dogs who can't learn new tricks.

6. Display Consistency

Without consistency, your goals will never become a reality. Without consistency, you will wake up every day with a sense of regret. You will never become the businessman, parent, spouse, or human being you want to be without consistency. Consistency is the piece that makes it all work.

It is that straightforward. As we get into accountability partners, we'll discuss how important they are in keeping your life consistent.

Failures and hardships and setbacks and sicknesses—they are all consistency killers. You've got to rise above and find people in your life who will help you stay consistent.

When you approach life consistently and make decisions based on a set of uniform values, your life has the most excellent chance of fulfilling your success definition.

7. Live with Integrity

I've told my family and my work family to, above all else, just be honest with me. I can handle any news as long as it's the truth. I might be upset, but I can handle it and we can move past it and figure out a solution.

Have integrity in everything that you do. I mean everything. You can't cheat, lie, or steal at any time in any situation, even if you're afraid that someone is going to reject you or choose not to do business with you. Without integrity, no one can trust you, no matter what comes out of your mouth. People will always question your integrity.

8. Be a Professional

Are you a consummate professional in the way you act, talk, and dress? If not, consider this: No matter what you do, you're always on stage. Whether it's a room full of people or just your spouse or kids, someone is watching.

I don't leave the house unless I am looking sharp because I never know who I'm going to meet. I don't go to an airport unless I'm in a suit, because I never know who I'm going to meet. That person could change my life, and that connection may have never happened if I didn't look professional.

No matter what you do for a living, looking and dressing like a million bucks is a good idea. It's always going to open up a conversation and suggest that you must be very successful in whatever you do.

9. Have a Strong Work Ethic

It doesn't matter how talented you are. What matters is your level of hustle—because hustle outdoes talent any day of the week. With the right amount of hustle, the talent always develops over time.

My son didn't play basketball until three years ago, and, when he first started playing, I told him, "If you want to get on the team, you're going to have to out-hustle everyone. Even if you have no skill, you have to be the first one to the ball and the first one up and down that court. Always."

If you can display any kind of work ethic in whatever you do, you're going to outwork and outdo everyone. Your competitors want something for nothing. They want to evolve with no effort, and that is how you can overcome them. Hustle!

10. Always Be Coachable

At the peak of their careers, legends like Lebron James and Tiger Woods still had a coach every single day. The best become the best because of their coaches.

No matter what level of excellence you reach in your career, you will always need a coach who can give objective critiques that you could never see for yourself. We make terrible accountability partners for ourselves, and we also make terrible coaches.

When you're not coachable, I don't want to work with you because you have proven to me that you don't want to evolve. You don't want to get better. You're not humble. Those types of people will poison the well in any business.

If someone forced me to pick the biggest reason for success in my life, I would say it's because I am coachable. I told you from the first line of this book that I stole everything that you're reading, and that is because I have allowed myself to remain coachable throughout the evolution of my life. I seek information and advice from others —those who are wiser and more experienced than I am.

No matter what level I reach in life, there's always going to be someone who is a level higher that I can aspire to reach. So, I want to talk to that person, and I want that person in my corner. No, I *need* that person in my corner.

When I progressed through the ranks at Allstate and built my business, it was all because I'd been coachable. I outworked everyone, and I had strong work ethic, but I also applied 100 percent of what other successful people told me to do, and I never questioned it. Then when I messed up, I took the initiative and asked, "What can I do better?"

Life is a game, but I don't mean that I don't take life seriously. It is just the opposite. Professional athletes view every game as the proving grounds, and I view every single day the same way. That is why I create my quarterly goals and then segment every year, month, week, and day into quarters. Then I take my goals, and I visualize them on my vision board—or the X's and O's on my playbook.

I approach every day as though I'm a professional athlete.

Did you notice that I never called myself the "coach" of my career? I would never pretend that I can coach myself to victory.

We haven't even scratched the surface on being accountable to others and remaining coachable yet (more to come in later chapters). Getting your idea of success outside your head is one of the critical elements of making things happen. Your vision board helps to accomplish this, but it can't stop there. You have to empower the people around you to hold you accountable as well.

Coaching, mentoring, and staying accountable are the next essential parts of developing a Success Psyche, which you'll read about in Chapters Seven and Eight.

Are you ready to crush your quarterly goals with tools like my goal-setting **GPS** guide? Put on your game face, and let's continue. And don't forget to visit *www.TheSuccessPsyche.com* to download your free copy of my **GPS** spreadsheet.

I OWN AND OPERATE A FEROCIOUS EGO.

BILL MOYERS

SEVEN

RESPECT THE POWER OF EGO IN ACCOUNTABILITY

Have you ever let yourself down?

Don't worry, I already know the answer. Each one of us has whispered that quiet, encouraging promise to ourselves in the darkness of our bedrooms as we drift off to sleep.

Tomorrow, I'll wake up early.

Tomorrow, I'll work out.

Tomorrow, I won't eat any processed food.

Tomorrow, I'll call 50 prospects.

Tomorrow, I won't get on social media.

Tomorrow, I'll read fifteen pages of a book.

Tomorrow, I'll do that project.

I'm sure you can add plenty of promises to this list. We can all relate to the feeling of making a silent promise to ourselves that, deep down, we know has virtually no chance of ever happening.

When we set *internal* expectations, what happens to the impetus to complete the task? It's just not strong enough, and, as a result, we'll let ourselves off the hook with virtually no hesitation whatsoever.

Getting your goal out there, outside your mind, and into existence —now *that* is when things get done. You've got to let people know. There is so much power in that.

When it comes to promises made to others, I've always been the kind of person who does what he says. I hate to admit it, but I once felt pride about being "wired this way." It was as if this somehow made me more special or better than those who were regularly disappointing their friends, family, employers, or clients by not living up to expectations.

"I'm a man of my word," I'd say smugly, secretly thinking that I must have more integrity than those *other* people.

When someone didn't live up to their promises, it made me upset. I wouldn't want to do business with them anymore, and I lost respect for them. But then I realized something one day. I wasn't special or had some deep, internal moral fiber superior to that of other people.

What I realized is I have a massive ego.

I realized that the only reason I was so adamant about doing what I promised was that I didn't want to look bad.

> **That didn't make me a unique, morally superior person. It just meant my ego was too big to allow myself to disappoint others.**

Once I realized that I wasn't unique for saying that I was a man of my word, it got me thinking a lot about ego and how it controls us. That's when I discovered that people live in an *egoic state* for their entire lives.

And maybe, just *maybe*, this isn't as bad as the psychology textbooks make us think it is. By the end of this chapter, I hope you'll agree. So, let's inspect the word *ego* a little more closely.

THE SURPRISING ESSENCE OF EGO

The term *ego* is confusing and overused. We use it to refer to a variety of different psychological concepts and processes. We also use it as a disparaging term when we talk about abrasive people or just straight-up jerks. People with big egos are no fun to be around, and people with superegos aren't worth being around at all.

You hear the word ego, and it definitely doesn't fill you with warm fuzzies, right?

But what does ego actually mean? What are psychologists really talking about when they use the term? And what did Sigmund Freud intend when he wrote about ego?

This may come as a surprise, but Sigmund Freud never once used the word ego in his writings. Not one time. Ego is the closest English translation scholars could identify for the German term Freud used in his work known as *das Ich*, which literally means "the I."

When Freud used the term *das Ich*, he was referring to the conscious, decision-making part that humans regard as "I." Ego is the person you think of when you take ownership of anything. (i.e., *I want to quit my job*, or *I love my kids*.)

> In other words, your ego is the *you* that you think of when you think of yourself.

Ego is "I," plain and simple.

There are ego or "I" thoughts and activities (ones that are based on your ego). On the other end of the spectrum, there are thoughts, motives, emotions, and behaviors that don't involve much ego (ones that aren't about "I").

When you have a conversation with a close friend, are buried in a great book, or get lost in a good TV show, those are examples of your "I" stepping into the shadows. The opposite of this type of feeling is what you see in highly depressed people. For various reasons (many of them they cannot help), people who are incredibly depressed are focused exceedingly on themselves and what is wrong with their "I." It's all about *their* personal experiences and no one else's.

So, obviously, there's got to be some sort of middle ground where we have "just enough" ego, right? Well, it seems that the world disagrees. In fact, when I was looking for quotes about ego in writing this book, I was struck by the fact that *every last one* of them was negative.

"Ego is the enemy."

"Shun your ego."

"Run from those who have an ego."

Based on our limited and inaccurate understanding of ego, I get what they're trying to say. But this is terrible advice when you really think about it. Let's figure out why that is.

ACKNOWLEDGE YOUR EGO TO UTILIZE IT

Remember when you were a little kid, and you were trying to impress your parents by riding your bike or scoring a goal? That's ego. We want credit for things we do well, and I don't see that as unfavorable, in most instances.

Pure *altruism*—or acting to help someone else at some cost to oneself—is about the farthest from ego that you can get. Let's be honest here: Unless you are Mother Teresa, you are getting some benefit from your daily actions.

Is this a bad thing? Not as long as your job is ethically sound, and people are better for having worked with you.

Within that context, the ego can actually be an incredible goal-setting and goal-*doing* tool in our daily lives. I came to this realization around the same time I realized that it was my ego that made me "a man of my word."

I can't stand the thought of someone thinking less of me. I can't bear the feeling of knowing I have disappointed someone else—and that's all my ego's doing.

When I realized that, I decided to start using the ego's power to my advantage by telling everyone all of the promises I was keeping to myself. For example, I decided to start getting up at 5:30 a.m. and told several friends and my wife about this goal. Then I gave them permission to hold me accountable. When I decided to take work operations to the next level, I told my entire team and my coaches, mentors, and friends.

I wasn't about to let down everyone around me. Just not going to happen.

Get your ego involved by getting your goals outside your head. Tell everyone your promises because, if you tell other people you like and respect, you will be much less inclined to let them down. Here is a simple example:

> Let's say you decide to lose twenty pounds in a month, but you choose not to tell anyone. Can you think of a reason why you would prefer not to tell anyone? If you're being honest with yourself, it's likely because you're really not serious about losing weight. So, fast forward thirty days, and guess who still has that extra twenty pounds? You do.
>
> Now imagine posting on your social media profile that you'll lose twenty pounds in a month, and you ask other people if they want to lose weight with you. Suddenly, you have a team of accountability partners who will be checking back in with you in thirty days to ask you if you've lost the weight.
>
> Which one do you think will help you lose the weight more quickly—your secret weight loss goal that no one will ever know about or the one that's out there for the entire world to see and has your ego involved?

We are *horrible* at keeping promises to ourselves. The sooner you realize this, the better. Expectations that you hold inside your own mind are next to useless.

Yet, the crazy thing about expectations is if someone *else* doesn't do something that we expected, we get upset and assign meaning to their lack of action. A great example of this is when a husband comes home and expects his wife to greet him with a kiss, but she doesn't. He gets upset and concludes she must not love him like she used to. Or when a wife expects her husband to magically know when she feels sore and would like a shoulder massage. Then she gets upset when she goes to bed without a back rub, even though the wife never once told her husband she wanted one.

Remember, the only people we can expect anything from are the people we pay money to and ourselves. That's it. But that doesn't stop us from getting offended when people don't do what we believe in our minds they should be doing.

The even crazier thing is that we develop all of these elaborate reasons why someone let us down. Then, we won't even do the *simplest* things that we promise ourselves! And instead of assigning our personal lack of follow-through a meaning, we designate it an *excuse*. We give it a "valid reason" that gets us off the hook with our ego.

"I am just too busy, and I don't have enough help."

"The pandemic made it impossible for our business."

"I can't stay on my diet because I'm traveling so much."

"I can't go to bed early because I've got too much work."

"No one is buying this product anymore anyway."

"My boss is not a good manager, so it's not my fault."

"My company didn't train me properly, so it's not my fault."

I've never met an adult who can't think of a million excuses for why they don't honor their commitments to themselves.

If this sounds like you, you're not alone. But just because everyone else has the same tendency doesn't mean you can continue (remember, "most people" is a terrible comparison benchmark). So, how do you stop making excuses and start using ego to your advantage?

Build an accountability system into your life.

I'm always telling people about my new ideas. I must bore some people to tears because I get so excited about ideas and love talking them into reality. Why do I get so excited? I enjoy putting my goals out in the universe to create accountability.

I've been telling a few friends about an idea my wife and I have for a business to help other couples called Empower Couple or EC Squared. When those friends and I talk, they always ask, "How's EC Squared coming along?" And it's the kick in the pants I need to make it happen.

Making that commitment to yourself and then telling everyone else that you possibly can about it? Now *that's* an idea that would make any ego proud.

QUALITY ACCOUNTABILITY IS KEY

After you tell the universe, take it a step further and give other people permission to keep you on track. Say something like, "If I don't live up to this promise, you need to call me out on it."

You can't get offended because somebody calls you out on an unful-filled promise or commitment.It's natural to go on the defensive in those moments. But it's best to fight the inclination by realizing your ego is just feeling a little embarrassed. Deep down, none of us want to let another human being down.

> **You're not really offended. You're just disappointed in yourself. Own that—and then do better the next time.**

Do hard things, and you will not have to feel offended or embar-rassed. It really is that simple.

Give people permission to hold you accountable and do a regular cleansing of those accountability partners because not all account-ability partners are created equally.

At the beginning of the 2020 lockdown, three of my friends and I committed to doing 100 push-ups and 100 squats every day, seven days a week, no matter what. We sent daily text messages to keep each other on track for the first month and a half. After those first six weeks, I was still doing my daily reps, but I noticed no one else was texting. I decided to wait two weeks and see if anyone else initiated a check-in.

No one did.

Finally, I sent a text, "Really weak, guys. We made a commitment to do this, and no one is texting now. What happened?"

Of course, everyone responded back with excuses, as well as some,

"Yeah, but you're not texting either," kinds of responses.

I shot them straight. "This is not what accountability partners do. They don't make excuses. They step up and say, 'You're right, and we'll fix it.'"

That is what accountability partners can do for each other. If your accountability partners enable your excuse-making, you need new accountability partners.

You need someone who will make you feel guilty if you don't follow through! Give your partners permission to say, "Does your word mean nothing to you?" However, you also need someone to celebrate your victories. You need both. I think about a good relationship with an accountability partner as a *love-hate* kind of thing. I *love* the fact that they keep me accountable, but I *hate* them (just a little bit and only when I'm messing up) because they're so good at calling me out when I'm slipping.

The worst accountability partners are the enablers. If you are trying to stop drinking and your friend says, "Forget about it tonight, and let's go grab a drink!" that's not a good fit.

If you want to change your life, you've got to change your way. And the only way to do that is to create new habits and then commit to people to stick with them. In other words:

> **You have to stop being a "Starting Monday" kind of person.**

How many times have you promised yourself that you will start a new habit on Monday morning? How many times have you kept that promise?

Ximena got me a Peloton for Christmas a few years ago, and I promised myself I would use it three times a week. Well, I didn't start using it. So, when I finally made the commitment and decided to make it stick, I began posting on Instagram every time I would take a ride. I'd post a screenshot of the display to hold myself accountable. It feels good to be able to send that screenshot every single time. My followers and my wife know I'm a man of my word, and I have a sense of accomplishment.

So, yes, accountability partners are essential. But don't depend on them to do the work for you. Ultimately it comes back to "I"—to the part of you that wants to be able to say, "I did this. I wanted to change my life, so I changed my way."

STOP CREATING CRISES

I hope by now you see that the ego can be such a useful tool in your life when you harness its power. There really are only two options: You can use it to your advantage, or you can allow it to sabotage you.

How many of the perceived crises that we experience in life stem from our egos? When we fail, we create narratives in our heads about how we will be judged, and, suddenly, we have manifested a crisis that didn't even exist.

A real crisis is a nuclear war. A genuine problem is a pandemic. But for the most part, the failures in our lives are *not* crises. I know there are exceptions. However, for most of our lives, we experience failures that we should be able to overcome quickly.

So, what happens? Why do we allow the failures (a.k.a. perceived crises) in life to completely derail us? It's that pesky ego again. We fail, and our minds internalize that failure. We think we "did something wrong," and we don't want to let people down again. So, we just don't try again. The feeling of letting others down is certainly not a feeling that anyone enjoys.

Well, guess what? Our egos also don't like letting ourselves down. So, all of those times when you've made silent pledges to yourself that you're going to get up early in the morning, but then you don't? Your mind starts to doubt that you really can or that you're really able to be disciplined.

> **You are self-sabotaging, one broken promise at a time.**

So, when a failure or some sort of career crisis comes along, your brain (that is used to you letting yourself down) immediately concludes, *I knew it! I knew this wasn't going to work.*

And that's the mentality that prevails in your life from that moment forward.

Here is a fact: Sometimes, you're not going to have the answer. Other times, you're going to find a solution out only by finding out all of the wrong ways to do it first. If you aren't okay with that, then you need to be okay with living a life of disappointment—because that is what you're going to have.

Get your ego on your side and start to use it as a tool by getting your goals *outside* your head and enlisting others' help. If your ego is anything like mine, then your desire to not let others down will keep you going when you would otherwise quietly accept defeat.

> **Ego is not "good" nor "bad." It only becomes harmful when you aren't aware of it. Once you acknowledge your ego, you are left with the benefits of its existence.**

I know this is not a health and wellness book, but let me add this: Your diet and exercise priorities tell you a lot about your ego's health.

Does your ego need a boost? I know that question goes against what modern motivational and psychological books tell us. Still, I firmly believe there are some people whose egos need a swift motivational kick in the butt.

The bottom line is that when you eat better, move regularly, and sleep well, you are a better spouse, a better parent, a better employee, and a better leader. So, one could argue that allowing your ego to help you make better health decisions (and career decisions) is actually an act of *selflessness*. Yep, I said it.

It's time to start reframing your mind about the word *ego* and seeing it as a tool rather than something to shun.

Your ego should not ever be your top priority. Don't mistake that as the message here. I am saying that it is an undeniable truth that our egos don't want to be embarrassed. They want to see us win, and we can use that to our advantage.

You've got an ego, and it's not going anywhere. So, you might as well get the most out of it. Retrain it to work for you rather than the other way around. Ego is "I," and guess what? It is that same "I" who is responsible for making the most (or the least) out of your life. It's not up to your upbringing or your parents. It's not up to your spouse or your boss. It's "I." Repeat after me:

> **I alone am responsible for empowering my ego by enlisting others to hold me accountable to reach my goals.**

After all, you can't spell accountability without an "I" (two of them, actually!). So, don't be ashamed to admit that you want it. Just hold your ego accountable by getting it outside your head.

In the next chapter, we'll talk about the kind of people you need to bring into the mix to help get you there with more accuracy and less frustration.

I ABSOLUTELY
BELIEVE THAT PEOPLE,
UNLESS COACHED,
NEVER REACH THEIR
MAXIMUM
POTENTIAL.

BOB NARDELLI

EIGHT

FIND MENTORS,
OR SETTLE FOR "GOOD"

The thought of bowling typically evokes a few thoughts in people's minds: childhood birthday parties, fat guys, tacky shirts, and maybe *The Big Lebowski*. But not for me. Bowling was just a normal part of life from the time I was three years old. My parents loved to bowl and played weekly, so I naturally developed a love for the game.

I played four sports throughout high school—basketball, football, baseball, and bowling. I was good at all of them, but I wasn't *great* at any of them, except for bowling. Let me tell you, I could bowl. For a short time, I even considered going pro.

But I did not want to give up any one of my sports, so I continued to play all four or them. If I would have focused on just one, I more than likely could have gotten a scholarship and gone on to play after college.

When you're trying to focus on too many things at once, that ironically creates the opposite of "focus." As a result, it's difficult to become *great* at anything.

You can be *good* at a lot of things. This was true for me when I left Waffle House to become an entrepreneur. At one point, I was running an insurance company, a mortgage company, and a real estate company. Then one day, I had an epiphany:

All of my businesses are doing well, but none of them are doing great.

After some consideration, I decided to take the insurance route because of the industry's residual aspect. In the real estate and mortgage businesses, you're only as good as your last month. I wanted to build something that provided income regardless of whether I was in the office or on a yacht.

There's no question in my mind that I could've been great at any one of those careers—but you can't bowl on three lanes at once, right? I had to pick a lane. I had to decide what I wanted, and I had to become laser focused.

To this day, I have never seen an athlete be the best in the world at more than one sport. A few have tried—but it just doesn't happen. When I realized this, I became determined that if I wanted to be the best, I needed to treat my business like a sport.

At the height of his career, you didn't see Usain Bolt training all day in track and field and then heading to the pool to work on his backstroke all night long. The most elite athletes pick a lane (a niche) and then become the best in that lane.

That is also what the most successful people in business do—with the help of a few essential people.

THE ONE THING ALL CHAMPIONS HAVE

Usain Bolt earned his fame by becoming the fastest man in the world. He probably didn't need a coach anymore at that point, right? How much faster can you get if you're already the fastest?

Usain Bolt doesn't see it that way—which is *why* he became the fastest man in the world. When asked about the importance of his longtime coach and mentor, Glen Mills, Bolt once said, "He has always made the right decisions for me. He is a guiding light in my career, and he has shown me the way to improve myself both as a person and as an athlete."

In professional sports, the difference between being the number one player in the world (recognized by everyone) and being in the top 100 (recognized by very few) is often a matter of mere millimeters or milliseconds.

> **There is this tiny fragment of a difference between the very best and all the rest.**

It's no different in your career. There are likely thousands of other people doing what you are trying to do with your life. How do you stand out in a sea of similar or maybe even nearly identical offerings?

Maybe you think the best get lucky. Perhaps you hear a massive success story and think, *That guy must have really lucked out,* or *She must have been in the right place at the right time.*

All excuses. That's your ego admitting defeat and trying to justify your failure after one too many times of you willingly forfeiting your unspoken goals.

If you dig deep, you will find that every single success story has one thing in common. That one thing spelled the difference between standing out and making a name for themselves and being just like the next person.

That thing? *They have a coach.* Coaches and mentors give you invaluable advantages you could never get on your own:

1. **Vision.**

   First, they provide you with a unique *vision*. The right coach can see what you can't see. You are too close to see the whole picture. They can help you take the necessary steps to back up and see the entire frame, assess, and figure out the best move forward. They also know how to get to where you want to be because they are already there. Without them, you are flying blind.

2. **Objectivity.**

   The next is *objectivity*. When it comes to your career, there is no one more personally invested than you. That's a good thing, but it can also be a problem. That problem stems from one word: *emotion*. Emotion clouds everything, and it can sabotage your best efforts. Coaches provide you with impartial, objective advice that can help you figure out your missteps more quickly and effectively.

3. Perspective.

Another benefit of having a coach is *perspective*. If you only rely on one view—yours—you are severely limiting your potential. Coaches force you to think about things in ways you could never do on your own. The right coach can provide a perspective that could help you avoid costly mistakes. Small course corrections from coaches have put countless dollars in my pocket. They have helped me redo my mindset and focus on real issues (instead of the perceived crises my ego creates).

4. Encouragement.

Coaches are your most significant sources of *encouragement*. They push you and challenge you. Even natural-born leaders are not immune to the slumps, funks, and motivation destroyers that plague everyone else.

As bystanders, we all thought that Usain Bolt had reached his peak. Again, how much faster can you get than "fastest?"

Well, here is what Bolt's coach had to say about that in an interview back when Bolt was at the height of this career: "I wouldn't say that we have seen the best of him. I think that he's capable of more ...."

The coach of the world's fastest man thought Bolt could be faster. He saw untapped potential in someone who, to the rest of us, looked like he was as good as it gets. That is both amazing and inspiring.

When you think you've done all you can do, your coach will pull more out of you than you even knew existed. When you feel you've reached a plateau, your coach will reveal the path to the next level.

PAY OR DON'T BOTHER

If you want to learn how to be the best at something, what do you do? Find someone who is already the best and do what they did. This really should *not* be a groundbreaking concept to anyone.

Coaches are everywhere now—they're like the roaches of social media. You can't go on social media without seeing some advertisement for a coach pop up who has all the answers you need. Maybe they do, and maybe they don't. But one thing those ads *do* get right is that no genuinely transformational coach should be helping you for free.

Remember, the only people from whom you can have expectations are the people you pay and yourself. If you don't pay your coach or mentor, you have no right to expect a single outcome from your time or efforts together.

Free is not going to help you. Ever had a free golf or tennis lesson? If you're anything like me, you got out of those lessons precisely what you put into them—nothing. I've had lots of free golf lessons, and I'm still a horrible golfer.

We pay for our son to have a top-notch basketball coach. We could have gotten lots of people to help him for free, but guess what? They would have been inconsistent, and they wouldn't have taught him the fundamentals. Most importantly, if they didn't make my son better and stopped showing up to help him, I would have no right to say a thing about it.

When you pay for something, someone's invested in you. A mentor's income is dependent upon you getting better at the thing you're paying that person to learn. That is an important point I don't want you to miss:

> **You are paying that coach or mentor, which means that person is your employee.**

People treat mentors like they're bigger and better than them, but they're not. They're an employee. That also means you don't let them dictate the rules—it's you who dictates the rules. You should be able to say, "This is what I expect. Otherwise, the relationship will end."

They aren't doing you a favor by allowing you to pay them for coaching. I've seen time and time again people make the mistake of feeling lucky because a coach "chose" them to be a part of their mentoring group. This is backward. You are paying them for a service, which means you are allowed to have expectations.

When it comes to coaching, the rule of thumb is "pay a little, get a little." You don't pay them a fee—you invest in yourself.

There was a prominent businessman who I'd met and wanted as my coach. I called him one day and said, "I want to learn everything from you."

The problem was he wasn't in the business of coaching or mentoring. "Well, I'm not for hire," was his reply.

I didn't miss a beat. "Everyone's for hire. What will it take?"

I told him he could name his price. He shot back with a figure that I'm sure he thought would make me run as fast as I could in the other direction. Instead, I didn't hesitate.

"Where do I send the check?" I asked him.

Surprised but impressed, he finally relented but added, "If we're going to do this, I have one expectation. Whatever I tell you to do, you do it as long as it's legal. If you don't, then I'm done."

I agreed but had my own stipulation as well. "Agreed, but I have an expectation for you. Whenever I call you, you pick up the phone. If I'm paying you this much money, I need to have access to you. Can you be available for me?"

"For that amount of money, yes."

You've got to be upfront with mentors like this. I've been to many seminars where a guy in a suit sells the pipe dream hard from the stage. The problem is that most "coaches" don't deliver. Once they get your check, that's the end goal for them. They have what they need from you, and you've been played. Sure, they'll throw some content your way to try to make you feel like you're getting your money's worth. But you know better.

The best mentors and coaches paid dearly for their knowledge, and now that knowledge is precious. I continue to rely on my paid mentors to help me take my business to new heights, develop personally, and foster a Success Psyche. You wouldn't even be reading this book today if it weren't for my paid mentors. So, just make the commitment to pay for coaching.

You've got to invest in coaching, but you've also got to find the *right* coaching. Don't even bother getting a coach unless they have the traits in the next section.

LOOK FOR THE RIGHT TRAITS

When we were little, we had coaches and teachers. When we were teenagers, we had coaches and teachers. We went off to college, and what did we have there? You guessed it—we had coaches and teachers.

Suddenly, once we graduate, the world decides we don't need coaches and teachers anymore.

I don't know about you, but I had precisely zero things figured out at age twenty-one. In fact, there was never a time in my life when I needed a coach *more*, and yet I was expected to figure things out on my own.

We're expected to build businesses and find the career of our dreams with no help whatsoever. This is nuts!

There is never a time in your life when you need to coach more than you need one right now. However, like everything else in life that comes with a price, not all coaches are created equally. So, what type of coach do you need to help you fulfill your own unique version of success? Here are the top four qualities to look for in a coach.

1. They have to have a niche.

First and foremost, you need a human being that's an expert in the field in which you want to become an expert. Back in school, every teacher or coach had their specific niche.

That's why you don't need a *life* coach—you need a *niche* coach.

When I hired my first mentor (the one who "wasn't for hire"), I found him after asking everyone I met, "Who's the best in the business?" This guy's name kept coming up. I knew when he said, "I'm not for hire," he wasn't trying to sell me. I was trying to sell him, and that made me want him as my coach even more.

If you hire a generic success coach, you're going to get generic results.

If you are in a specific industry, find someone who has the answers within your industry. Would you hire a coach who specializes in health and fitness to grow your tech start-up? You could, but you are not going to get the specific answers that you need.

Find a coach whose successes in your industry you admire greatly. You've seen where they came from and what they've done, and you want to do what they did. Those successes will inspire you, and they will also give you some specific benchmarks to work toward.

2. They have to be honest with you.

A good coach will always shoot you straight. They're going to call you to the mat and be completely honest with you. You're not paying them to build you up; you're paying them to tear you down and make you better.

You need to hear comments like, "Get your head out of the sand! What are you doing!?"

Coaches get paid millions of dollars in professional sports to tear players down and build them back up. They're not out there to stroke players' egos with comments like, "Oh, Tom, you're just such a great quarterback. You're so good looking and talented. Keep up the good work, champ!"

That's not what a great coach does.

You can buy more success books after this one, and, believe me, I know the benefits of a good book. However, a book is not a substitute for a coach. A book can't stand over you and hold you accountable. A book can't give you a good kick in the pants when you need a kick in the pants and give you the honest feedback that will make you grow.

3. They have to allow you to set expectations.

Speaking of books, you also can't have grand expectations from a book. You can expect a book to provide you with ideas that you then are responsible for executing—ideally under the watchful eye of a coach or mentor.

Coaches who are worth paying for are confident enough in their coaching abilities to allow you to set some expectations for them. If a coach is unwilling to abide by a few ground rules, that is not the coach for you.

Taking that a step further, they have to give you permission to check back in with them to see if those expectations are being met. Of course, they should give you both positive and negative feedback along the way, and you should be able to do the same.

When you find a coach who doesn't have any problem with that, that is a person who will live the journey with you and be in your corner. You don't want someone who's going to plug you into their generic "proven system" and try to use the exact same formula they used for the last person. You are not a number, and your success definition is unique. If they are not willing to acknowledge that, then they are not the coach for you.

4. They have to fit with your style.

This book is my perspective on success because it's based on my own experience and daily mindset. But these concepts won't work for everyone—and I'm good with that. In fact, I expect this to be true because we're all so different.

You can read the same chapter twice and get something completely different out of it based on your mood and what is going on in your life at that moment. For this reason, you have to ask yourself what you are really looking for in a mentor or coach.

I look for someone with a personality similar to mine. Someone who is wired the way I am wired. And there is one thing I can say about all of my coaches over the years: I can relate to their experiences, trials, and errors in a personal way. Their success story moves me, and it feels like it could be my story as well.

If you find someone who has a style you can emulate, it can make the journey a little better or at least more straightforward. It's not a prerequisite to have a coach with a similar personality to yours, but it may help enhance the results.

LEARN TO NEGOTIATE

There's one skill that you need before you hire your next coach. I'm talking about the ability to negotiate.

Some people seem born to haggle, while it's the stuff of nightmares for others. I'm not talking about price haggling. I'm talking about "haggling" for the right expectations and laying the proper groundwork.

Think about the last coach you hired. Imagine if you had said to him or her, "Let's do this for ninety days, and let me see if I work for you and you work for me."

The best coaches won't hesitate.

Learn how to negotiate for the things that you want, not for what they're trying to sell you. There's someone out there who will be willing to work for you and put their money where their mouth is.

If someone is unwilling to go on trial for a few months and prove themselves, I immediately suspect that they are not men or women of their word. I instantly assume that they will not stand behind their empty promise of results.

When you're dating, it can take a few months to determine whether there are just too many differences for it to be the right fit. The same is true with coaching. That's why any mentor worth a hefty investment should be good with you saying, "Let's date (so to speak) for ninety days and see if this is something that's going to work for both of us."

This type of negotiation creates a win-win for everyone. After those ninety days, if you are happy with the coach's work, you will be fiercely loyal. And they know that they have developed a relationship that will benefit not only you, but also that you will likely tell others.

Every new employee that comes to work for me knows he or she has ninety days to shine. It's that type of pressure that brings out the best (or worst) in people. Believe me, coaches want you to stick around, and the motivated ones will agree to a trial.

When I was looking for a company to help me create a set of core values for my business, I found a firm called EOS. I wanted to work with them, but I also wanted to negotiate the work on my terms.

I didn't want to travel with my whole staff down to Texas, so I asked the founder to come to me. She agreed but charged me more. Fine by me. If you don't ask, you'll never know what someone may be willing to do.

I took it a step further. The company charges a sizable daily consulting fee, so I asked if there were any business opportunities or referrals that I could provide to lower the investment. The founder stood her ground. "Absolutely not. That's our price."

That made me want to work with them even more.

Then, she added that I wouldn't even have to pay if I didn't think it was worth it. There were no contracts beforehand or pre-payment. She had a hefty price tag but backed it up with some big promises.

There were no gimmicky lines like, "Pay in the next fifteen minutes, or you lose this special price!"

There was no 100-page long contract where I'd be locked in for a year with a colossal retainer every month.

There was no price hassling or "incredible deals" where I supposedly get $10,000 worth of value for just $499.

None of that nonsense.

What did I have to lose in this situation? Absolutely nothing! I only had potential gains.

At Agency Sales Academy (our coaching platform for insurance agents), we don't have contracts. If you want to leave at any time, you are welcome to leave. We don't want anybody to pay for something in which they see no value. If you came to a live event and didn't like it, we'll refund your money. No questions asked.

Negotiate terms you love from the start, and then communicate throughout the process, especially if you feel your coach is not holding up their end of the bargain. Just remember, when you make these types of deals, you have to hold up your end as well.

My once-reluctant mentor told me I had to do everything he asked, and if I didn't, I was gone. This was fair, and it set the right expectations.

Too many people are afraid to negotiate. There's this strange stigma in the coaching world where people feel like they're applying to work with someone and, if they're lucky, the coach will take their money.

Think about how ridiculous that sounds.

Stop letting people sell you on the "sizzle." Get all of the "steak" worked out in the contract, and then commit to your end of the deal.

ASK THE RIGHT QUESTIONS

Negotiation is not all about getting the absolute lowest price possible. It's about negotiating the terms so that they set you up to win. I'm talking about setting expectations and creating a trial period to make sure there is a fit.

Coaches claim they are the best. What are they willing to do to prove it? If you have to pay them upfront with no money back and no guarantees, I can guarantee you one thing: They are *not* the best.

A key to successful negotiation is asking the right questions. One of the biggest reasons I've had success in my life is the questions I ask.

Ask if they would be willing to do a month-to-month contract or one for ninety days. Never sign a contract that locks you into a commitment for a year or more without first asking if there is another way. A year is too long, at least until you know whether the partnership works.

There's no question that you should never ask.

I don't care if it's personal. Ask it. Before I work with the coach, I want to know if they've ever been unfaithful to a partner. If they are willing to cheat on someone they love, they'll have no problem cheating on me.

I don't work well with people who do certain things, so I need to know before paying them money.

There is not a question I won't ask about a person's business. *How did you do it? How much money did you invest in getting where you are today? How much money do you make now? How much money have you lost?*

Take their contracts and pick them apart. Ask in specific terms what you can expect to get out of it. The agreement should not be all about them—there should be a clear understanding of the work they will do for *you* and the tangible results you can expect.

If the contract doesn't make it clear, ask questions. If they don't want to answer, that is their right. And it's your right not to work with them!

WHATEVER IT TAKES

When people ask me how many mentors they need, I tell them as many as it takes.

Because you need a mentor for each niche, it's impossible to have just one mentor while operating with a Success Psyche.

- I have a mentor for my insurance business.
- I also have a mentor for real estate investing.
- I have a mentor for mergers and acquisitions.
- I have a mentor for my health and fitness goals.
- I have a mentor for my personal life.

I pay every one of these people, and they're worth every dollar.

I'm also a mentor to my employees. I'm "on stage" with them all the time, and they receive my direct feedback. I learn by interacting with other mentors what not to do as a mentor myself. When I see a style or a tactic that repels me, I vow never to do that.

Of course, there are always going to be people who don't like my style. The best mentors are going to have haters. If you have haters, you're doing something right.

As a matter of fact, I like haters. I once used to focus on them. I'd get 300 positive comments but concentrate on the one negative one. I'd think, *How dare you say something negative about me!* I used to erase the comment and block them. Now, I gladly engage them in a conversation to see if I can turn them around.

Let's not forget about how ego plays into all of this. Remember that when a great mentor agrees to work with you, they're putting their ego on the line. They don't want to let you down, and you shouldn't want to let them down either. Although no one can truly "get rid of" their ego, you can acknowledge that your ego is there so that you can set it aside and remain coachable.

The best coaches are coachable as well. You should be able to give them feedback on the job they're doing. What are they *not* giving you that you need? What techniques are they using that you *love*? If your coach has too big of an ego and is not aware of that ego, the coach will not accept feedback. And that is not the coach for you.

Ultimately, you have to decide what you want in life. No coach can do that for you. You have to determine what you want and then find a coach to help you get there.

I had a decision to make when I was eighteen years old. I could have chosen to pursue professional bowling. If I had, I would've found a coach to help me make that dream come true. But that wasn't meant to be my path. I wasn't meant to be "Jay Adkins, Professional Bowler."

I figured out what I wanted after a lot of searching in the wrong places, and my path revealed to me the types of coaches and mentors

I needed along the way. And, since then, I have never stopped seeking them out.

There is comfort in the fact that someone from somewhere has already done what you are trying to do. Someone else figured out how to fail and succeed and can give you the advice you need to avoid some of the roadblocks.

No matter who you are, where you've come from, or what you have achieved, a good mentor is an invaluable business asset. Zig Ziglar couldn't have summed it up any better: "A lot of people have gone further than they thought they could because someone else thought they could."

Find someone who believes you can reach further than you could dream—and let them help you find the path to massive success.

INTENTION WITHOUT ACTION IS AN INSULT TO THOSE WHO EXPECT THE BEST FROM YOU.

ANDY ANDREWS

NINE

DISCOVER THE DANGERS OF GOAL MYTHS

People set a goal. They don't reach that goal. They conclude they are destined to fail. They give up.

Rinse and repeat.

Goals are tricky. How much is too much? How much is not enough? Goals are supposed to stretch you, but they're also supposed to be attainable. They have to be big enough to *seem* unattainable ... but also doable ... but also scary.

Well, at least that's not confusing, right?

Let me go ahead and cut to the chase: Setting and attaining goals is not easy, at least not at first. Fortunately, it's a skill that you can significantly improve upon the more you do it. Goals also become much more straightforward once your Success Psyche is in place.

Still, what is a *goal myth*, and why are we doing another chapter on goals after we already covered my **GPS** *(Goal Planning System)* in Chapter Six? Because goals are too important to limit to only one chapter. It's time to get honest about what goals are and what goals are not. We need to discuss what mindsets are standing in the way of you setting and reaching your goals consistently each quarter.

Consider this to be a preemptive goals-troubleshooting guide so that when you fail, you don't default to your old programming, throw your hands in the air, and conclude, *I knew it!*

There are nine goal myths that block success. As the chapter title indicates, these myths can be dangerous when they are not dispelled through conscious effort.

MYTH 1: SETTING GOALS IS THE KEY.

Goals can create a cruel illusion of success when you believe that *setting* them is the same as *acting* on them. Still, that doesn't stop people from setting goals that they have no intention of pursuing.

When those goals fail to somehow magically accomplish themselves, there is almost nothing more draining. It is profoundly demotivating to watch goals fade away unfulfilled.

That is why *setting* a goal is not good enough. The act of picking a goal is only one small piece of the puzzle. I've known a lot of unhappy, unfulfilled people who set goals. In fact, setting goals and then not achieving them is one of the fastest ways to block your Success Psyche development.

You can avoid the trap of setting but not actively *pursuing* goals by developing a system. Everything that functions well and produces results in my life does so because it runs on a system. So, it should be no surprise that I set goals systematically. As we discussed in Chapter Six, here is what that system looks like:

- I create four to seven business goals and four to seven personal goals every ninety days.
- I design a vision board for both on *www.PhotoCollage.com*.
- I print out my business vision board, put it on my bathroom mirror, and set it as the wallpaper on my devices.
- I print out my personal vision board and put it on the refrigerator.
- I plan the exact **GPA** (*Goal Producing Activity*) required to hit my goal.
- I set this **GPA** on my calendar as a reoccurring appointment.
- I write my daily goals every morning during mindset mapping.
- I evaluate my progress every Monday and make adjustments as needed.
- My family has a weekly meeting every Sunday to discuss our personal/family goals.
- I move any incomplete goal to the next quarter as a top priority.

I know this system may not work for everyone, but it's been life-changing for me. The most important thing is to develop a plan that keeps your goals top of mind. If you set goals and act upon them daily, you're going to see massive gains. That's an undeniable fact. And if you choose not to take action, then what you have are not goals—all you have is a useless wish list.

MYTH 2: I FAILED BECAUSE THE GOAL WAS TOO HARD.

If you fail to complete a goal within ninety days, it's okay and even expected (from time to time). The problem is that most people give up.

Instead of giving up, become a detective. Figure out why you failed. Don't accept any loss at face value because there is always more to the story. What does it mean if you fail to accomplish one of your goals? Among other things, it could mean you didn't:

1. Remind yourself daily or do a weekly evaluation.
2. Tweak your goal as the quarter went along based on your progress.
3. Base enough of your daily actions around that goal.
4. Prioritize your goals.

For any goal that I failed to complete in a quarter, I carry it to the top of the priority list for the next ninety days. Each quarter must have its priorities because it's impossible for all of your goals to carry equal weight or importance. This is another reason why "less is more" when it comes to goals. Let me explain that by asking you a question:

Which one would be more encouraging for your psyche: to set four goals and accomplish them all or to set eight goals and accomplish only half of them?

It's much easier to prioritize a shorter list. Keep yourself laser-focused every quarter so that you can accomplish *all* of your goals. Then start fresh again the next quarter. This promotes a sense of accomplishment that acts as a significant motivator—and this creates impetus.

Results motivate action!

In most cases, the real underlying reason for not completing a goal is that it was not a priority for you. So, you have to ask yourself: *Why did I include it as one of my goals if I had no intention of actively pursuing it?*

Asking honest questions like that is how to differentiate goals from pipe dreams.

MYTH 3: DREAMS ARE GOALS.

If goals carry over a second or third time, then it's time to consider that they're not goals, or at least not top priority goals, for you at this current stage in your life. You need to then reassess and determine, "Is this truly a goal, or is this just a dream?"

The dreams you have when you sleep are not attainable. You wake up, and they don't exist. *In ninety days, I want a Bugatti* is a fun dream. However, that's an immature goal and one that doesn't naturally lead to actionable steps.

Be realistic, but test your limits a bit. Goals should be attainable—but they should also make you uncomfortable. If people don't laugh at your goals, they're not big enough. The naysayers should respond to your goals with, "Yeah, right. That's never going to happen."

One thing to mention here is that dreams still matter and are not meant to be ignored. Just don't confuse dreams for goals. Don't dream it. Do it.

MYTH 4: COMPARISON IS MOTIVATING.

The world tells us to compete against each other, but, when it comes to comparing goals, a comparison may cause you to end up chasing someone else's life. Comparing your goals to those of someone else will do one of two things: It will either limit your potential or overwhelm you.

What do *you* want to do? What do *you* want to create? Your bliss journey is yours and yours alone. It doesn't matter what other people's goals are.

Michael Jordan did not set goals based on what other basketball players did before him. If he had, he would have only ever been *as good* as them. Instead, MJ created his own benchmarks—levels never before reached by another player. That is how he became the greatest of all time.

If you want to use someone else's success as a benchmark, then at least set your sights *above* them rather than striving to equal them. Create your own version of success. Blaze a trail!

Until 1954, no one thought a human could run a mile in under four minutes. For years, four minutes was the accepted standard— the peak time. That is, until Roger Bannister clocked a 3:59.4-minute mile on a windy, rainy day in England, unlocking the physical and psychological door that everyone before him thought would remain closed forever.

My wife loves the NBC show *America's Got Talent*. A few seasons ago, I watched a dance troupe audition with moves I had never seen before. If they had made a goal to be *just as good* as dance squads from previous seasons, I wouldn't even remember their performance. However, they crafted their own version of success and, as a result, they created an unforgettable experience for viewers.

Set your goals based on what *you* want to accomplish, not based on what anyone else has done. Instead of thinking, *I want to close ten new clients a month like my colleague Bob,* tell yourself, *I want to close fifteen new clients a month ... like me.*

You aren't doing it for your boss. You aren't doing it for your spouse. You aren't even doing it for your kids. Ultimately, what you accomplish may benefit them. But you're doing it for yourself.

It's time to raise the bar and set some new standards.

MYTH 5: PRAISE IS MOTIVATING.

There is one thing about goal setting that never changes: You can't rely on others' praise to keep you motivated.

Don't expect recognition, because it might not happen the way you envisioned it. You may be thinking to yourself, *I can't wait to hear what my wife says about my huge accomplishment.*

But when you tell her all about it, all she gives you is, "Nice job."

That's it? You put in all those hours for a "nice job?"

You cannot predict what someone is going to say or think about your accomplishments. That means it can't matter what anyone else says or thinks. You have to ask yourself, would this goal still be worth it, with or without a compliment or recognition? If the answer is yes, then it's a goal worth pursuing.

And what if you accomplish something significant to you but somebody mocks it? Some of our fellow humans seem to love tearing down others. Maybe they're secretly jealous, or maybe they're just jerks. Whatever the reason, you cannot allow them to become your kryptonite.

> **Don't let the voices *outside* your head become the voices *inside* your head.**

The bottom line is that when we try to be successful for other people, it doesn't work. What if you accomplish a goal and don't get the response you were looking for? People rarely react the way you think they're going to react. I've experienced this many times. I'll tell my wife or a friend about an accomplishment, and I have this whole scenario planned as to how they'll respond.

But it never plays out that way. Ever.

It shouldn't be about my wife's reaction anyway. It should be about what I'm doing for myself to become a better husband, father, employer, and human.

As an employer, I have even witnessed recognition become a demotivating force. A few team members received praise, and, as a result, they took their foot off the gas and failed the next quarter when it looked like they had it all figured out. Meanwhile, other team members have become resentful when they didn't get the accolades that they thought they deserved.

Recognition based on expectations is a slippery slope. You have to learn to be pleased with your success apart from any exterior accolades. Stop looking to what others will give you and do the hard things for yourself.

MYTH 6: THERE ARE SHORTCUTS.

The way people create success is by setting goals and focusing on them. Pretty simple, right? What makes it more challenging is when discipline has to get involved. Of course, step one is to create a system or a plan, just as we've discussed. But, as Mike Tyson once famously said, "Everybody has a plan till they get punched in the mouth."

The mouth punches are coming. If you haven't been punched in the mouth yet, then I question whether you are actively pursuing meaningful goals. If you are determined to accomplish a particular goal, you must be willing to do whatever it takes.

There are no shortcuts in life. If you want to get stuff done, it's time to get productive. People mistakenly think they're productive because they're busy. But what they are really doing is *appearing busy*.

Ask yourself, *Am I engaging in frenzied activity or a Goal Producing Activity?*

Do the things you don't want to do. Playing a game on your phone instead of reading a book is not going to get you there. Hitting the snooze for the fifth time instead of getting up and starting your day is not going to get you there.

> **All the things you don't want to do are what it's going to take.**

The hard things are the things that change you. Those are the things that are going to skyrocket you to your goals and your success.

It takes a lot of effort to sit down every morning and map out actions that are not a waste of your time. But what is even the point if you don't? Why continue to operate without a **GPS**?

Here's a little secret: I don't like writing stuff down. I don't like doing it—and that is how I know I need to be doing it. Legendary health and fitness guru Jack LaLanne once said, "If it tastes good, spit it out." I feel the exact same way about activities: *If it's easy, don't do it. If you don't want to do it, do it.*

When I don't feel like getting on the Peloton, I get on the Peloton. When I don't feel like reading, I read. When I don't feel like getting up early in the morning, I jump out of bed.

> **The feeling of *not* wanting to do something is my trigger to do it.**

Find your trigger! Just remember that finding your trigger requires you to stay in the present moment. Most people live for the future, and you can tell it by the way they talk:

I can't wait until this weekend.

I can't wait until my next vacation.

I can't wait until this project is over.

We live so far into the future that we are wasting the present.

Part of the problem is our culture of instant gratification. As a society, we expect it all *now*. A worthwhile goal is not going to be instant—but I'll tell you what *can* be instantly gratifying: Doing the hard things at the precise moment when you don't want to do them.

Whenever I feel that please-don't-make-me-do-this feeling, that's my trigger to act. And I'm always glad I did. I feel accomplished and productive, and that creates the *impetus* I need to do more challenging things.

Here is another critical differentiation to make—*momentum* is not the same thing as an impetus. Momentum comes and goes. All you have to do is stop moving, and all of that momentum is lost. But impetus? That's what gets you moving again, even when you feel frozen in place.

The unfortunate tendency most humans have is to procrastinate. We look at a goal with a ninety-day window and think, *Great, I have three whole months to get this done.*

The first month goes by—nothing.

The second month goes by—nothing.

We get to that final month (or the last week of that final month) and feverishly try to reach the goal. Inevitably, we fail. What does this due to our psyche? It crushes it!

Discipline and *consistency* are the tools needed to break this vicious cycle. Chip away at your goals in the same way that you would eat an elephant, and you'll get a seismic amount accomplished over time. You're going to see a compound effect, and the payoff will be incredible.

Only you will notice the change at first. Then your family will see it. Then your work colleagues will notice. Eventually, the whole world will notice. By then, your life and your path will be forever changed, and you'll realize that the present moment is where it all takes place.

MYTH 7: A CARROT IS BETTER THAN A STICK.

Do you have consequences in place for not attaining your goals? Without setting up consequences, the only thing you will experience after failure is regret. Regret is a powerful consequence, but it's also demotivating and plays right into our failure programming.

People tend to believe that rewards (carrots) are more motivating than consequences (sticks). But really, you need both. Set up consequences, and then tell people the consequences for failing to meet specific goals. Make it hurt. No goal, no dinners out. No goal, no vacation. If you set a consequence that affects others (such as no family vacation), make sure there is a consensus among those affected.

When you tell a child there will be consequences for misbehaving or failure to do a task, but you don't follow through on enforcing it, that kid knows you're not serious. In the future, your son or daughter has no impetus to behave. Similarly, when you fail to accomplish a goal, and there are no consequences, your brain recognizes that failure is acceptable and expected.

There must be consequences when you don't keep promises to yourself. If you are in one of those moments, here are some key questions to ask yourself:

1. What will not reaching my goals cost me?
2. How will I suffer and who else will suffer as a result?
3. What will my life look if I fail but then give up?
4. What will my life look like when I succeed?
5. How will being successful improve build my character and relationships?
6. How will success improve my finances, health, and happiness?
7. Who can I inspire to create success by creating my own?

Don't let your brain become complacent. Hold yourself to a higher set of standards by holding yourself accountable. Since you are a *terrible* accountability partner for yourself, tell other people about the consequences and let them help you be a person of your word (a.k.a. your ego).

MYTH 8: MOTIVATION COMES FROM OUTSIDE INSPIRATION.

What motivates you? Do you even know? I'm not asking what inspires your family or what motivates your friends or your favorite Instagram influencer. I can't motivate you, and your spouse can't motivate you. Motivation comes from within. In fact, the point of this book is not to motivate you but to *inspire* you.

> **Inspiration comes from the *outside* in an effort to change you on the *inside*.**

Motivation ultimately comes from within, and the way you get motivated is to take action. If you wait until you feel motivated to act, you'll probably never act. If you're not taking action, you're not going to see results—and what motivates us is those results. We take action … we get a result … that result encourages us to continue. It's counterintuitive, but that's how it works.

A notable difference between unsuccessful and successful people is that when successful people experience failure after taking action, it does not demotivate them. Instead, that failure motivates them to continue.

> **Do you wallow within failure, or do you persevere through it?**

You have to figure out not what motivates you but what *inspires* you. Then, you are responsible for taking that inspiration, internalizing it, and producing the action that leads to results. Motivation is temporary, which means that your impetus to act must come from a source within you.

Failure is a subconscious belief system from which you must break free. When you become conscious in the present moment and act, permanent failure is not even a possibility. Failure may be something that happens to you along the way, but it doesn't stop you in your tracks. You pick up the pieces, dust yourself off, and keep moving.

MYTH 9: SOME FAILURE IS OUTSIDE MY CONTROL.

Whenever you fail, there's only one reason: you.

Nobody else can create failure for you. If you blame the economy, it's a cop-out. You could blame a pandemic, but that's just an excuse. If you blame your employees, well, you hired and trained them and accepted less than "excellence." So, whose fault is that?

There is a universal truth in life you must hear, understand, and accept: *The problem solvers make all the money.* I am talking about inventors, visionaries, presidents, and CEOs. The problem solvers win, while the problem makers stay broke and disappointed. Problem makers always work for somebody else because they can't (or aren't willing to) work independently. If they did, they would have no one else to blame for their failures.

Own your failures. The buck stops with you because that's the only way that you can take control of your destiny. If you're not asking the right questions and being honest with yourself, you can't take control of your present or your future. Ask yourself:

What motivates me?

What inspires me?

What would I like to create in my life?

What does my ideal future look like?

As you achieve your goals quarter after quarter, don't forget that great things take time. The beautiful masterpieces and great architectural wonders of the world took years to complete. Athletes who have sculpted bodies and superhuman skills work tirelessly to achieve results. People who build billion-dollar businesses put in countless hours of blood, sweat, and tears to reach that level of greatness.

Even then, they are still continually failing. These problem solvers just aren't whining about it all the time, so we simply aren't aware of their missteps (the same thing can't be said about problem makers, who are always complaining).

The one thing you can control is the fact that you can always dream. A dream may not be the same thing as a goal, but dreams *can* help you create goals that work to make your dreams come true.

If you were to Google "goal setting techniques" right now, you'd be flooded with advice—some great, some not-so-great, and some terrible. Somewhere out there, every answer you could ever need for how to attain your goals already exists. Yet, more and more people are struggling to achieve their goals. What is it that's causing this disconnect between knowledge and achievement? A few reasons may be:

- There are too many opinions (analysis paralysis).
- There are too many naysayers in our lives who belittle us and discourage us from taking risks (thus perpetuating our failure programming).
- There are too many fakers (people portraying false pictures of success).

We live in a filtered, fake world that is full of negativity. Combine that with the limiting beliefs ingrained in you from childhood, and it's an uphill battle to fight the good fight and take action.

Do you know the best remedy for lack of action? It's action.

I know—seems a little obvious, right?

Then why aren't you doing it? This book is about so much more than a mindset. It's all about taking massive action. It's about being a doer rather than a talker.

Are you going to fail in the pursuit of your goals? You bet you are. Embrace it. And if it doesn't hurt a little (or a lot), then it's not an action worth your time. Do the hard things, and you'll cross those goals off one by one each quarter!

THE CURRENCY OF REAL NETWORKING IS NOT GREED BUT GENEROSITY.

KEITH FERRAZZI

TEN

PRACTICE THE NINE BE'S OF NETWORKING

S ome things in business have remained the same over the years. Relationships are still king. Smiles open up a lot of doors. And integrity is vital to long-term success. But one thing that has changed in the last few decades is networking. Since the pandemic, networking has changed even more.

Most of the networking advice out there right now is absolute garbage. Actually, it's been garbage for a long time. For years, people have been getting it all so wrong. It's more than meeting a group of people for lunch and exchanging business cards. It's more than following up a networking meeting with an email telling a prospective customer more about you and what you do. It's more than adding someone to your LinkedIn connection list. It's more than liking posts of someone whose business you want to earn.

Networking needs to be a process. It also needs to be extremely intentional.

Successful networking requires outside-the-box thinking. It's a part-time job in and of itself and one that you cannot ignore or outsource to much of a degree. If you plan to be a mainstay in your business, you must understand how to correctly utilize social media. Because what's happening today on social media that people call "networking" is frankly an insult to people's time and intelligence.

Every day, I get lazy attempts on my socials to connect. You can't do the networking everyone else does and expect anything valuable in return. You must use tools other people typically don't use. Don't just "like" a post of one of your prospects or customers. Comment and engage them via insightful, exciting questions.

Use the tools out there to your advantage.

Start conversations!

Note I did not say use *people* to your advantage. Because we need to set the record straight right now. People are not tools. People need your help. Yes, you need them, too. But if you approach life with a *what can I do for others?* attitude in all interactions, the results will astound you.

As this chapter's title suggests, there are Nine Be's to becoming a great networker. But all of them are useless without first deciding to create a relationship with someone to see how you can help *them*—how you can help them personally and how you can help them in their business. Make it about them.

1. BE CURIOUS.

The most effective way to build relationships and friendships is to "leave people with themselves" every time you have a conversation. My grandfather taught me how to leave people with themselves when I was bussing tables as a teenager. He explained that I could make more money and make more of an impact by giving people a *gift*—not a tangible gift but a feeling you leave with them.

You accomplish this by asking questions.

Getting to know who people are and asking more than, "How are you?" doesn't have to be time-consuming. Don't be shy—be curious!

Rather than only asking what they're eating or if they'll be needing ketchup, I asked questions that made guests understand I saw them as people rather than a tip. My grandpa told me to ask what they were celebrating. If they weren't out for a special occasion, ask them what they'd *like* to celebrate, what the highlight of their day was, or what they hoped to accomplish that week.

Most people don't really care about other people. It's tragic but true. If you can show other people that you care about what they have to say, you'll be miles ahead of everyone else. It's a surprisingly easy way to stand out because most people don't fight the tendency to let their egos take over and make everything about them, them, them.

Think back to Chapter Five, when I asked you about the last time you saw a group picture that included you and who you looked for first in the image. Of course, you looked for *yourself*, and the reason goes back to ego.

And, yet, caring about others (I mean *really* caring) is everything in life.

If you are always the one asking questions, you can build relationships very quickly. Whenever I meet anyone new, I ask at least five to seven questions about them.

- I want to know what they do.
- I want to know what their day looks like.
- I want to know one thing they would change about what they do.
- I want to know what they love about what they do.
- I want to know how they see their future.
- I want to know about their family.
- I want to know what they love to do for fun.
- I even ask them how much they make in a year. (Crazy question, right? Well, most people will tell you).

Even if I don't know anything about their hobby or passion, I can still ask more questions to show that I'm genuinely curious to learn more.

Questions are important because they gather information, but it's even more than that.

How can you know until you ask? *You can't.*

And if you don't learn new things, how can you solve the situations that become your obstacles or roadblocks? *You can't.*

And it's more than just asking—it's also listening. Like Steven

Covey said, "Most people do not listen with the intent to understand or learn. They listen with the intent to reply."

Don't be that person who is impatiently waiting for your turn to speak. Listen to understand and learn. Become that kind of listener, and people will love being around you. They may not even know why, but they will want to talk to you again—and again. But you'll know why. It's because you made them feel heard. You didn't rush them so you could chime in and sound important.

Think about one of those rare moments in life when someone asked you a question and then actually listened intently while you responded. How did you feel in that moment? That same feeling is what grows relationships and, it's the secret to building a killer network.

2. BE RELATABLE.

My life experiences have been rich and varied enough that, unless their interests are highly unusual, I can relate to almost anyone about something they love. Whenever possible, leverage your experiences that relate to theirs. Being relatable shows people that you are on their side—that you *get* them. When I relate to others, I keep it brief. I don't go into too much detail about my story unless they ask.

Think about how many random things about you of which very few people are aware. Those kinds of things are engaging and relatable! Here's a random one for you:

I learned how to drive a forklift when I was sixteen and worked in a lumber yard. I was tired of picking up boards and drywall. It was back-breaking work, and there was a forklift sitting right there, ready and willing to do the heavy lifting.

So, I would sneak away and practice driving in the back of the large yard.

I became so skilled that I finally got to drive the forklift every day. It was a much better job than manual labor. I had acquired this skill that made life more comfortable, and it was also meant to come in handy a few years later.

When I got deployed to Dhahran while in service to my country, I was miserable. Finally, we got word that we were going home, but there was a caveat. The forklift driver was in the hospital, and we couldn't leave until he got better—or they got someone else to drive the forklift to load all of our gear and equipment.

I quickly shot up my hand. "I know how to drive a forklift."

My commanding officer was surprised. "But you're an IT guy who works on airplane avionics. What do you mean you know how to drive a forklift?"

I replied, "I learned how to drive one in a lumber yard when I was sixteen."

"Yeah, but this is an industrial forklift."

"No problem," I said. "That's what I learned to drive."

Everyone else wanted to get home as badly as I did, so they gave me a shot. I worked eighteen hours straight on that forklift and got us the heck out of Saudi Arabia.

I've lived a full life with unique experiences—and I'm guessing you have as well. And we all have our versions of the "forklift story" that we can use to relate to and connect with others.

When you listen and then share brief anecdotes (that have nothing to do with your business), and you leave people with themselves, people walk away thinking, "Man, I really like that person."

They may not even know why they like you, but you'll know why: You've given them a gift! You've "left them with themselves" and had a pleasant conversation that made them understand you care about what they have to say.

> Just be kind. It's not that hard, and it's free.

Carve out time to find out about other people and relate to their stories in some meaningful way. When you care about someone's day and relate to them, that's when a genuine relationship can form—and form quickly. Being curious and relatable are two of the most incredible ways to speed up your pace in building a network.

3. BE CREATIVE.

The next important aspect of effective networking is engaging in follow-up activities. Fortunately, social media has made this much more straightforward. It's easy to send a quick note via someone's social profile, and it's less invasive than old-school methods. You don't have to try to get them on the phone (and interrupt their day), and you don't have to text them and face the potential awkwardness of them not texting you back. Even email has become a cesspool of junk messages, and notes can often get lost in spam folders.

Be careful not to let the ease of connecting with others on social media lull you into complacency. You still have to put in work. Don't just send a friend request. Add a custom note and include relevant things that you know about them. Better yet, send them an audio message. After you're connected, don't merely "like" their pictures, comments, or links. Contribute something useful to their posts.

I'm also a fan of sending quick video messages. These don't have to be lengthy or elaborate. You could just say, "Hello my friend, I hope you are doing awesome. It would be great to see you and connect, so let's go play some golf or grab a coffee, dinner, etc." This is much more personal and memorable than a text message, and it will help you stand out from the crowd.

I am also a stickler for sending friends and contacts a birthday text. I might sing "Happy Birthday." I might rap or beatbox a birthday message. Whatever it is, I guarantee that it's going to be different from what other people are sending.

Don't be afraid to stand out by being creative.

4. BE SYSTEMATIC.

The best networkers have a system for how they connect with everyone. I keep a digital journal of people I need to reach out to regularly. I even have a list of people that I text every day and people that I call weekly.

I schedule my phone calls during my daily commute because it feels like a great use of my time. I can fit in five or six conversations on my way to and from the office.

When I make a call, I always give a disclaimer that I just have just a few moments to talk. They are busy, and you are busy, too, so set a precedent at the beginning that you are just checking in quickly.

This is also important: Don't make any sort of "ask" when you call to check in on them—just reach out for the sake of seeing how they are doing.

Create a system for what you are going to say and how often you will call each level of your contacts—from friends and family to prospects and new and long-time clients.

There are people you will naturally talk to weekly, monthly, quarterly, and yearly. You get to decide what the frequency is, but, whatever you do, decide on a systematic approach for making contact and stick with it.

> **To keep your network alive, you have to touch base with them regularly.**

I saw a colleague who posted about losing a lot of weight. At the time, I hadn't talked to him in six months. So, I took that opportunity to tell him how great he looked. Then, I brought up some conversations from the past about work opportunities. He was actually still interested in those opportunities, which benefited him. It also re-opened a door for me that would've otherwise remained closed.

5. BE AUTHENTIC.

I know the word *authentic* gets thrown around a lot, but it's imperative to be yourself, especially in the social media age. Everyone can see through tired gimmicks, and the old sales tricks just don't work anymore. Sadly, people really don't know what *authenticity* is anymore. That's because most are living a lie on social media, pretending to be something they are not.

We do this because of our ego (once again). Our ego is what drives us to be inauthentic—we are afraid of other people's judgment if they see our flaws.

It can be daunting to consider becoming more authentic. The most straightforward place to start is to be authentic with yourself. If you're not true to yourself, you will never be authentic with anyone else. It begins with you. Every day, we lie to ourselves and break internal promises. We make excuses and try to justify those broken promises.

Stop the vicious cycle by being honest with yourself, and that honesty and authenticity will naturally flow into others' lives. Never try to be something you are not. We all have skill sets, and we all have imperfections. When we're not authentic, people sense it. On the other hand, if people perceive your authenticity, they will stand in line to do business with you.

6. BE OPEN-MINDED.

I'm always intrigued to meet new people. After I meet you, I'm going to make a decision, based on my network, as to whether you'll be a yearly, quarterly, monthly, or weekly contact. I rarely meet a person from which I cannot find any mutual benefit in maintaining the relationship. However, if you bring negativity into my space or judge me, you're not going to be in my network. It's not worth it.

I'm passionate about my family, my career, and helping other people. That means I want and need people in my network who share my passion for life. We don't have to have the same beliefs or the same interests.

> **Passionate people can relate to other passionate people—no matter how different they may seem.**

You can be passionate about your beliefs without alienating those who feel differently. If you are prone to shutting down those who think differently from you, you're going to miss out on relationships that will positively impact your life.

We miss out on so much when we can't express our true feelings.

I'm authentic; I want to attract other genuine people into my life. I know what subjects are sensitive for some people, and I respect that. There is never a black-and-white issue when it comes to relationships. They're messy—really messy (the good ones at least).

7. BE CARING.

Building a valuable network takes a particular skill that far too few people possess—and that skill is *care*. You've got to care about people. You have to ask questions.

I met a man who stood out to me (for all the wrong reasons) at a Tony Robbins business mastery event. He was one of the most selfish people who clearly only cared about himself and what he could get out of a relationship. There was no two-way street. There were no questions about someone else.

Those people—the ones who only want something from you—are so obvious. We all see them coming from a mile away.

Like any other skill, caring about people is something that you have to actively work toward improving. You'll know when you've mastered it because you'll have lots of real friends, lots of contacts, and lots of messages—and a whole lot of people will want to be around you.

> People who are caring attract others because we all want to be around people who care.

Caring could mean just being a good listener. If you want to be successful in business, you're going to have to "die to self" and genuinely consider others. Do that, and everything else falls into place.

One of the easiest ways to show you care about someone else is not trying to sell them anything. Just get to know them. After you have built trust, there will be time for you to tell them about what you do. If you start a relationship to get as much out of it as you can for *you*, it will never be a valuable relationship.

Care about people. It's so simple, and it's so effective.

8. BE VALUABLE.

Antiquated sales techniques and "perceived networking" (i.e., connecting with others solely for your own gain) are dying, if not already in the grave. Today's networking absolutely necessitates that you provide value to other people.

I created a concierge program when I first started my business, and I still use it today. Back when I had no money and lived in my car, I obviously also had no money for marketing. In those days, billboards, radio, and TV were the only forms of marketing.

There was no Internet, and the print options all came with hefty price tags (with not enough return on investment). We each have around 22,000 subconscious thoughts a day, and when we pass by a billboard, we quickly move onto the next thing in front of us and forget all about that static message we just saw.

I needed a way to stay top-of-mind and be valuable enough to people that they would think of me whenever they thought of insurance. My concierge program was born out of the need to network in a way that benefited everyone involved and provided real value to people.

Here's how it came into existence: A good friend was a concierge at a posh hotel in New York City. At the time, I had no clue what a concierge was. I had been poor my entire life, and I'd certainly never been in a five-star hotel. In fact, the "fanciest" hotel I've ever stayed in was a Fairfield Inn.

My friend invited me to visit her, and when I arrived at her hotel, she was standing behind a counter in the large, palatial lobby. I watched as she helped some guests find the best places to eat and decide what entertainment they would enjoy that evening.

After they walked away, I asked her how much she charged to help those people (I had seen them hand her money).

"Oh, that? That was just a tip."

"Well, what do they have to pay the hotel?" I asked.

"Nothing."

I was shocked. "Why would the hotel do that? That seems like a lot of work for nothing."

She replied, "Because we want to make guests' experiences amazing, and we want them to associate that feeling with our hotel. Because I made everything so easy on them, they'll come back and book with us again. That's the reason for the service."

And that's when I had an epiphany. I needed to be doing the same thing in my business!

I had struggled with providing tangible value to my customers because what I sell is an intangible product. At the point of sale, I sell nothing more than a promise. I'm promising that if you get into a car accident, you will not have to worry about the financial burden of that. You're walking out the door with that promise and nothing more.

I wanted to offer more than just a promise. So, I started visiting businesses and talking to the owners. Here is what I told them:

> *I want to give my customers more than just the promise of coverage. I want them to have a database of the best doctors, lawyers, doggy daycares, CPAs, contractors, mortgage brokers, real estate agents, veterinarians, and pediatricians. I'm building a network of trusted providers in every industry—places where they can be guaranteed excellent service.*
>
> *So, I want to advertise your business to my customers, and it's not going to cost you a dime. The only thing you'll have to*

do is provide me with a stack of 8½ x 11 flyers each month that promote your business. I will hand those flyers to my customers at the point of sale.

As you can imagine, this concept was extremely popular in my community. When I went to my concierge partners every month to pick up their new stack of flyers, I would take that opportunity to ask them how *their* business was going, and guess what? Most of those businesses became customers as well.

Thanks to Zoom and the Internet and social media, the concierge value-building type of service looks a lot different today—but it is still entirely possible. You can easily create a page on your website to provide links to trusted providers in every industry. Your customers will know they can go to your site for valuable deals and reliable business recommendations.

A great way to add to your list of valuable businesses is to ask customers for their recommendations for the area's best companies and services. Then, you have a way to call up those businesses and say, "We have a mutual customer in common. John Q. Client told me he had such a great experience with you. Well, we're looking to add businesses to our concierge program, and it's not going to cost you anything. You want in?"

This is a great way to build community, provide value, and add to your own prospect list.

I teach my teams to build two relationships a day. Whether that is on Zoom or in person, show people how you can help them in more ways than just what you can sell them.

9. BE PATIENT.

It takes time to build a healthy network full of valuable, positive contributors and a solid group of influencers. Especially when it comes to social media, it's not always easy to tell which techniques deliver tangible results. You will not typically see a direct sale from a Facebook post. However, the touches and activities build upon each other and work to create your reputation as caring and trustworthy.

Take the long-game approach.

Don't get impatient, and you will see great results from the relationships you foster. I wait several months before I even mention my business to most people. After ninety days, I'll call a contact and check in with them. Then I add, "Tom, I can't believe that I've been working with you for three months, and I've never asked you who does your insurance."

Obviously, that statement works in my business. But I don't care what business you're in—this can and will work for you, too. Here are some other examples:

- "I can't believe we've been talking for ninety days, and I've never asked you who does your hair."
- "I can't believe we've been talking for ninety days, and I never asked you what the interest rate is on your mortgage."
- "I can't believe we've been talking for ninety days, and I haven't told you about some of the houses I have listed or what we do at our real estate agency."

- "I can't believe we've been talking for ninety days, and I haven't told you about my restaurant or our catering arm of the business."

Don't make the mistake of going into networking thinking about what *you* can gain. When you take the concierge approach and help people, good will come back to you tenfold. And this applies to far more than just sales. This type of mentality will work in any business and across industries.

I don't remove anyone from my network unless they have been a negative influence or dishonest. Everyone I meet has value and becomes at least a once-a-year contact. Keep that person in your pipeline because you just never know. You may need them, or they may need you.

Perhaps the most valuable thing that you will get from your network is a constant stream of referrals. When you are a ninja networker, referrals flow in almost naturally.

However, that doesn't stop me from asking for them. I know many people are afraid to ask for referrals, but if you have been providing value to someone all along, there should be no fear in asking them to provide you with a name.

Look out for other people, and that's the fastest way to build a strong network where good is reciprocated. Be a person of your word and send other people business. Take the initiative and do it consistently, and people will be more apt to do the same for you.

There are many pieces required to create a Success Psyche. But without a network to grow your reputation and your business, the rest of them are useless.

"Your network equals your net worth."—Tim Sanders

I HAVE DEVOTED MY LIFE TO UNCERTAINTY. CERTAINTY IS THE DEATH OF WISDOM, THOUGHT, CREATIVITY.

SHEKHAR KAPUR

ELEVEN

EMBRACE UNCERTAINTY OR ACCEPT COMPLACENCY

Some things are easier to admit than others.

I have no problem admitting that I love sweets, but I also know better than to eat much sugar (other than whipped cream on my coffee ... stay away from my whipped cream). I also would never hide the fact that I don't like getting up early, but I still do it.

However, I never enjoy admitting that I woke up wracked with anxiety and stress for many years (and often still today). I once went to bed feeling overwhelmed, and I got out of bed feeling overwhelmed. There was so much I wanted to accomplish that I felt guilty when I didn't finish everything on my list. As a result, I woke up the next morning already feeling behind the eight ball.

I didn't realize at the time that I was pointlessly grasping for a sense of certainty.

I wanted to feel *certain* that I was healthy. I wanted to feel *confident* that I was doing the right activities to grow my business. I wanted to feel *sure* that I was building the financial freedom I desired for my future. I wanted to feel *certain* about my marriage and relationships.

Thanks to my daily reading time and meditation, I came to the slow realization that certainty doesn't actually exist. What's that famous line? "The only things certain in life are death and taxes." We've all heard that before and laughed—but it's true.

I also have heard that you have to "get comfortable" with uncertainty. Is it just me, or does that seem like one of those ideas that sounds great but is actually really hard?

Yeah, it's tough.

However, I know that to successfully develop a Success Psyche, you have to *relentlessly* do the hard things. Every day. The reason this is so important is that it is actually uncertainty that *creates growth.* Uncertainty creates drive. Uncertainty also fosters a sense of the unknown, and that is what makes you feel alive.

When you're certain, that's when you die. Certainty represents the death of your dreams and the death of the life that you picture for yourself.

FIGHT TO STAY AT THE TOP

Think about some of the most successful people who faded into obscurity over the years, never to be influential again. Their irrelevance came when they got comfortable. They got overly confident about their income and quit the hard work.

This happens all the time in professional sports. Without keeping their proverbial eye on the ball and practicing like they're still trying to make the team, athletes fade into obscurity. Another group of hungry newcomers will outwork and therefore out-skill the players who are coasting.

It's blatantly apparent which actors and actresses still practice their craft. The actors who have a wide range and can play any character —those professionals never stop learning. Then you have actors who get pigeonholed into one style or one character, no matter the film. Maybe the superstars just have more natural talent than the character actors. Or perhaps the multi-faceted actors just outwork everyone else.

What I do know is that unless you want to get pigeonholed, you'd better be ready to work.

When you get to the top, it's a fight to stay there. There is no easy button once you get to the peak. It's steep and treacherous, and there is no guarantee that you'll be able to hang on up there.

The sooner you realize that the better.

The key is to embrace uncertainty. You never know when the next pandemic is around the corner. You never know if you're going to make it home from vacation. You never know if someone else is going to sideswipe your car at eighty miles per hour. If another Great Depression is going to hit our nation. If World War III is around the corner.

There is really nothing that you can control outside of your willingness to embrace uncertainty. Sadly, however, the allure of certainty is the downfall of most people. One reason is that people are always striving for things that are not possible. They set big goals but don't reverse engineer them to figure out how to actually *reach* those goals.

If you set a lofty income goal but don't actually have a plan (your **GPS**) for how you're going to reach that number, you might as well set a goal to walk to Mars.

People don't reach their goals and then quickly give up. They conclude that uncertainty is too scary and too disappointing (never acknowledging that they refused to plan, be consistent, or think outside the box). They are content to crawl back into their unsatisfied little holes and do just enough to get their paychecks.

When COVID-19 hit, uncertainty was everywhere. Every conversation in 2020 was tainted with discussions of the pandemic and all the changes it brought into our lives. It also brought the downfall of many businesses. One of those was Nieman Marcus, who filed for bankruptcy in 2020. But here's the thing: It really wasn't the pandemic that did them in—that was just the straw that broke the camel's back. Nieman Marcus was already on the brink of collapse because of its outdated business model.

Big box stores are quickly becoming a liability. With all of that real estate, the steep rent, and the massive number of people needed to run operations on the ground, it's just becoming an investment that is too risky for many. It's also a model that is not going to survive for much longer. Every year, more people shop online, and fewer people go into stores. Nieman Marcus' entire reputation was built on their in-store experience. They had no clear plans for how to transition into creating that same sort of experience virtually.

When businesses get comfortable, they don't do the things needed to stay ahead of trends. Changing once something is *already* trending is too late.

The classic example is Blockbuster. They were so sure they had a grasp on the market. Then Netflix happened. Fast forward to today, and there's an entire generation that has never even heard of Blockbuster. Meanwhile, Netflix is now making big-budget, blockbuster movies (ironically).

WHERE ARE YOU LIVING?

Uncertainty fosters creativity. When you wake up and feel the twinge of that uncertainty, that is when you put your game face on, and you are ready to fight the next battle. When I wake up, I still feel the uncertainty, but I've conditioned myself to be excited about it.

Yes, excited! Because I know uncertainty is what keeps me creative.

Uncertainty is not valuable unless you trust the process. Many times, when I'm stressed, I think, *Why can't this just be simple? Why have I not reached my goal?* When I refuse to allow those thoughts to derail me or cause doubt to creep in, the next thought that pops into my head is almost *always* a good idea that helps me get closer to my goal.

If I was comfortable in certainty, I wouldn't be thinking that way. I wouldn't allow my creativity to get stimulated first thing in the morning as I role-play different scenarios to overcome various obstacles.

When I wake up with uncertainty, I smile and think, *This feeling means I need to think about this. I need to figure out another way. This is the process. Trust it.*

Instead of complaining, *Why can't I just wake up and feel a peace about this?* be thankful that you don't have certainty. It's that lack of peace that will push you to the next level.

Life equals uncertainty. As soon as you get comfortable, as soon as you feel confident about one thing, another will crash and burn.

The "if only" crowd definitely doesn't make the most of uncertainty. We all know the "if only" people:

> *If only I had $20 million in the bank, I would never have to stress about anything again.*
>
> *If only I met the right person, I would be happy for the rest of my life.*

The "if only" scenarios in life are illusions. Time and time again, people get their "if only" wish but are dissatisfied moments later. Or something comes along and knocks them out of the temporary comfort their "if only" brought.

During the pandemic, I checked in on one of my most successful friends, who is highly invested in real estate in the form of rental property.

"How are things?" I asked him.

He sighed. "I've never had so much stress in my life. I didn't get paid from 60 percent of my renters last month, and this month is not looking any better. I was so comfortable for the last five years. Now I have no idea what I'm going to do."

This was a guy who had it all together. He was always so sure about life. I told him, "You know what? This could be a silver lining."

He failed to see how most of his renters not paying could be a silver lining, but I continued.

"I know you may not want to hear this, but uncertainty creates greatness. Right now, you're thinking, *How do I survive?* You got comfortable because you built a real estate portfolio that was paying you. But now this uncertainty is going to make you think outside the box."

Outside-the-box thinking helps you get past those *I can't believe this is happening to me!* moments in life. What if you lose your job? What if you get sick and can't work, and then you have thousands in medical bills?

Life happens. Are you ready? There really is no way to prepare for all of the unexpected things in life because they are, after all, unexpected.

But you can decide that you will not be *consumed* by the fires of life.

Let those fires instead forge greatness in you.

No one wants to be around a martyr—they wallow in their situation once their blessed certainty fades away. Martyrs blame everyone else when things go wrong. Don't be a martyr. Embrace uncertainty and figure out how you're going to get through a situation rather than feel stuck in it.

Only 1 percent of the world's population has notable success. The reason is that this small percentage consists of the people who embrace uncertainty—and they know it's the ingredient that will push them on to the next step.

As we've discussed before, most people live in only one of two places. They either live in the past (which fosters regret) or live in the future (which promotes fear). Uncertainty scares us because we have a tendency to project the worst-case scenario into the future. But if you really think about it, the vast majority of the "terrible" things we just know are going to happen—they never actually happen.

Even if a worst-case scenario does happen, there is always a way out and through it!

To live with regret is to live in the past. To live with fear is to live in the future. Being present is the only way to create the brightest future for yourself and others that you'll impact. It's to live in the moment.

UNCERTAINTY CREATES YOUR LEGACY

It's way too easy to get complacent once you think you've arrived.

Then you get punched in the face, and it doesn't feel like you ever arrived. It's also way too easy to reach some destination and forget the *why* that got you there.

We have such short memories when it comes to pain, and that is both good and bad. It can be useful because it allows us to get back up on the bike when we fall down. It can also be harmful because we quickly forget all of the work it took to get us to where we are today. I invite you to let the battles and the knockdowns keep you humble and help you remember where you came from. I encourage you to recognize both the struggles and the triumphs.

> **Never forget the struggles because, if you do, you are destined to repeat them.**

Don't let comfort become a trap. When your workouts aren't making you sore anymore, work out harder. If it becomes easy to reach your income goal every month, it's not a challenging enough goal. Stretch yourself and become uncomfortable. Embrace uncertainty or become complacent (and eventually obsolete).

A big part of the uncertainty puzzle is being consistent. I know firsthand that consistency can be a struggle, and it's a struggle we all face. It's hard to be consistently kind to our spouses and listen to them. It's not easy being a consistent leader or team member and doing consistently excellent work.

It's all a struggle, but that just means that the end results are so worth it.

If you want to know whether you are embracing uncertainty, one of the best indicators is whether people are asking, "How did you do it?" If that has started happening to you, use that to your advantage.

People ask me regularly what the ingredients to my success are. There are many separate pieces, but I always tell them that my uncertainty mindset keeps me sharp. There's no shortcut to success—you have to do the hard things, be consistent, and have a positive mentality.

As morbid as this thought is, I have sat at funerals and thought to myself, *I sure hope someone says something like that about me one day.*

Have you ever thought about what you want someone to say at your funeral? I want people to love how I helped them improve their lives. My purpose on this planet is to help make people better, and I hope I'm known for assisting them to think outside the box and realize that they had more inside of them than they originally thought.

As you mentor and coach others, remember the pain and the struggle it took to get to where you are. Once you lose sight of that struggle, you're going to get comfortable, and that leads to the complacency that will be your downfall.

Don't become another Blockbuster. Face uncertainty and create your own revolutionary ideas and legacy.

Lots of people become stifled by uncertainty and give up. Those same people are going to tell you it's not worth fighting for your dreams. They only tell you this because they don't have the strength to fight for theirs.

Focus on the massive action right now, and the now will take care of the rest. When you have purpose, you will outwork everyone with ease. You will have a "whatever it takes" attitude even when you get knocked down. Remember, trust the process (the T in FEET). When a sacrifice doesn't feel like a sacrifice, this is when you have found your why.

Someone will always be waiting on you to give up. And maybe you will fail—but that doesn't mean you have to stop. Hard work, consistency, the right psyche, and resiliency will get you past the fear of uncertainty every time.

There will always be uncertainty about the future—but understand that uncertainty often turns into doubt—and that is where you start to get into trouble. Doubt is the worst enemy of determination and persistence.

The past is in the past, and the future is not yet here. What you have is the now. Stop allowing uncertainty to turn into doubt! This will happen naturally when you believe in yourself—because if you don't believe in yourself, nobody else will believe in you either.

Nothing will serve you more than believing in the you that you are today and believing that the uncertainty about tomorrow keeps you sharp and ready to fulfill your goals.

THE SECRET OF
HAPPINESS, YOU SEE,
IS NOT FOUND IN
SEEKING MORE, BUT IN
DEVELOPING THE
CAPACITY TO
ENJOY LESS.

SOCRATES

TWELVE

GAIN THE HAPPINESS ADVANTAGE

f I work hard, I will be successful, and once I am successful, I will be happy.

In the last chapter, I confessed that I used to wake up with anxiety. Well, I've got another confession: *I believed that first sentence for most of my life.* Eventually, I learned it was a lie—a horrible, destructive lie. In fact, the lie that "success breeds happiness" has done more damage to the collective happiness of our friends and family than almost anything else.

For years, I assumed that once I reached a certain "level" of success, I would be happy. I wasn't sure what or where that level was, but I figured I'd know it when I reached it. Then I read a book called *The Happiness Advantage* that changed my life.

In it, I learned that happiness is not a "mood" you stumble into or magically earn through enough victories. It's a *work ethic*. It's a way of approaching life rather than a destination on a map. My realizations about happiness and its profound role in our lives are so important that I've made happiness the final anchor point of my entire message. And for this reason, the takeaway I wish to focus on during our last chapter together is this:

> **We become more successful when we are happier and more positive, not the other way around.**

Happiness is a feeling that we have *as* we are striving for success. It's not the feeling that comes *from* that success. We've got it backward, and that has caused so much anguish and sorrow. Look at what pursuits get most of our mental energy and focus, and it's not hard to understand why so many people are miserable.

If the "pursuit of happiness" fails, then that perceived failure equates to failure in life.

This is such a dangerous and destructive mindset.

However, when we reframe failure as an opportunity for growth, that is when we will actually experience that growth. Happiness is a byproduct of our mindset. That means we can achieve happiness at any point in life, not just at some mythical destination in the future.

Happiness hardwires our brains to perform. Try to get quality work accomplished when you are negative or even neutral. It's such an uphill battle! When we are happy and positive, we are smarter and more motivated.

Happiness is the center, and success revolves around it.

LIFE IS A PRIVILEGE

After reading the book, I realized that I could experience the *happiness advantage* by seeing everything as a privilege. The fact that I get to experience failure in my business is a privilege. I genuinely mean this. The losses I have experienced over the years have led to my greatest successes.

The mere fact that I live in America is a privilege. No matter what's going on politically or economically, it's a privilege to live in the U.S.

I've always enjoyed volunteering, but I appreciate it even more since I redefined what happiness can and should be. If you don't believe that you already have everything you need to be happy, go volunteer at a children's cancer hospital. Go feed the homeless. Build a home for someone who doesn't have one. Volunteer to collect shoes for children who have no shoes.

Do you have food? Do you have shoes? Then what are you complaining about?

Now, I know it's not that simple. And I know that we need more in life than food and shoes. The point that I hope you do not miss is that whatever you spend your mental energy focusing on is going to become your reality.

One of the most significant parts of success is giving back and helping people.

If you are hungry but can't afford to eat, I'm going to buy you food. It's not because I'm some saint (because I certainly am not). I've simply been given the privilege of having the means to care for others, and, when they ask, I will provide for them however I can.

Now, I'm not going to just hand you a burger and be on my way. If someone accepts food from me, they'd better be ready to have a conversation. A few years ago, I saw a young man digging in the trash at a gas station. I watched him as he found a McDonald's bag and proceeded to pick away at what was probably a few French fries in the bottom of the bag.

I had to intervene. "You hungry?"

"Man, I'm starving."

There was a McDonald's next door, so I said, "Let's walk over there," as I pointed to the restaurant.

As we were standing in line, I wanted to figure out how he had reached a place in his life where he was looking for food in a trash-can. "So, why are you here? What happened?"

My hungry friend started making excuses as to why it all happened. Of course, nothing was his fault, and everything in his life had been "done to him." He was addicted to alcohol—and probably drugs, too, based on the look of his eyes and teeth. Still, he only confessed to the alcohol, which I already knew from his breath anyway.

I grabbed his arm with enough pressure for him to pause his story and said, "Hey, man, how old are you?"

"I'm 36."

I continued. "Listen, I don't care what substances are in your body right now. I want you to know that you were not put on this planet for this. God put you here to impact lives, and that's why

246

you met me today. I'm going to get you some dinner, but then I need you to sober up and change your life."

We had a great conversation that night. I've never forgotten that young man, and I hope that he hasn't forgotten me either, or at least hasn't forgotten what I told him.

How can I ever know if I helped him to find a better way? I can't. What I *can* do is have more conversations like that with as many people as possible. And I don't just mean people who are dumpster diving for food. I mean you. I mean my kids. I mean the young lady who bags my groceries. We all need to know that we were put here for a unique purpose only we can fulfill.

Go volunteer somewhere and see what's happening in other people's realities. The world needs more volunteers—people who are willing to step up and use their time, energy, and talents to help others. You do that, and the time you spend on your career and your life will be so much more beneficial and, frankly, so much happier. Living and working from a space of gratefulness and happiness is the most freeing feeling you can have in this world.

REGRET, FEAR, AND THE PRESENT

If you're happy in this moment, wherever you are, and with however much or little you have, then I believe you will achieve whatever you set out to achieve. Success will come readily to you. That is because happiness is the key ingredient! Yes, you need the other massive action steps we have discussed in this book. Still, once you gain the *happiness advantage*, something beautiful will happen:

You will be able to easily define success on your terms.

You will stop with the needless comparisons. You will realize that you *are* enough, and you don't have to act like or be like anyone else to live the life you've dreamed of living.

Regret plays a considerable part in the ability to be happy with where we are. Because so many people live in the past, the tendency is to stew in past failures. To relive them and never forgive ourselves. The choices we made, the choices we didn't make, the anger we displayed towards someone, the relationships we've ruined. If you think about it, it's pretty easy to live in a state of regret. It's easy to wallow.

But if you have regret, you can't have happiness.

I lived with regret for five years after my mother died. I regretted not spending more time with her. I felt I didn't do enough to help her in her final years. What I finally realized is that I am not a doctor. I wish that I had flown up more often to see her, but what good does that wish do for me now?

At some point, you have to forgive yourself and move on with your life. More importantly, you have to learn from your failures and do better at the next opportunity.

What about living in the future? Is that better? Absolutely not. The "I'll be happy when" crowd is the most miserable bunch I know. They also seem to be the same people who play out "what if" scenarios in their heads. I have been a "what if" person in the past and still struggle to fight the tendency (which stems from my desire for certainty).

What if something terrible happens to my family?
What if the economy goes south?
What if my team quits?

We set ourselves up for failure when we create catastrophe narratives in our minds. We're really good at it, too! Our "what if" scenarios become elaborate Greek tragedies within the confines of our imagination. It's amazing how creative we can be when we're thinking about a potential disaster.

Well, I don't know about you, but 99 percent of my worst-case scenarios have never happened. And when they have, I have figured out a way to move beyond 100 percent of them.

Why do we torture ourselves? Worrying about the "what ifs" of the future is different from planning and setting expectations for the future based on reality. Don't use happiness as an excuse to stay where you are. You can be *happy* but also be *driven*. The two can and should co-exist.

I've said it before, but it deserves to be repeated:

> *To live with regret is to live in the past. To live with fear is to live in the future. Being present is the only way to create the brightest future for yourself and, more importantly, for the others you will impact.*

Do you have some big goals for your life? Are there people that you want to impact? Well, you can't influence people's lives if you're unhappy. You just can't.

NERVOUSNESS IS NOT UNHAPPINESS

People often misinterpret feeling nervous as feeling unhappy.

When people say they're nervous about going on stage or getting on a Zoom call or about trying anything new, that nervousness tends to create unhappiness. The end result is never good: You either don't enjoy the experience, or the nerves and perceived unhappiness stop you from taking action at all.

Nervousness does not have to equate to unhappiness. When you understand where those nervous feelings are coming from, you will see that nervousness is actually a *great* thing. Feeling anxious, after all, just means that you desperately want to avoid letting other people down.

As you can guess, this once again comes from a place of ego.

One of my employees recently told me about her terrible social anxiety. This young lady also happens to sing at a large church. So, I asked her, "How do you get up on stage and sing in front of hundreds of people, but you can't have conversations one-on-one?"

She thought for a moment. "Oh, I don't know. I just feel like they're into the music, so it's not about me."

I responded, "Well, what makes you think it's about you when you're walking by someone on the street or having a conversation?"

"Because I feel like they're judging me."

"Do you know where that comes from?" I asked.

"I have no idea."

Most of us don't even know why we feel the way we do. She perceived her nervousness as some sort of social anxiety over which she has no power. She had no idea that her social anxiety came from a place of ego.

Acknowledging that ego is the first step toward taking away its power. When you say you're an introvert, that is more than likely not the case. That's just your narrative. That's the story you created to stay in your comfort zone. It's easy to get out of obligations by using the "introvert card."

You may or may not agree with me. Still, I hope you can at least acknowledge that whatever you keep telling yourself over and over again is what you become. When you convince yourself that you are an introvert and cannot put yourself out there, people are missing out on you. People aren't going to be impacted.

Whenever I hear someone say, "I'm just shy," I think to myself (or tell them if the timing is correct), "You're not shy. You're just comfortable. And you don't want to put yourself out there because you don't want to be judged. That's all ego."

This anxiety is not something we are born with—it's something we learn. At some point in your childhood, someone (or lots of people) judged you and made you feel self-conscious. Because of those past experiences, you became an adult who refuses to put himself or herself out there.

I don't think there's anyone who would deny that we have a tendency to judge one another. We look at other people and evaluate what they're wearing or saying. People do the same to us, too.

But not as much or as often as you think.

Spoiler alert: You may have an ego, but so does everyone else. That guy or gal you met at the networking mixer? Their egos attempt to keep their minds entirely focused on themselves. What you say and do doesn't matter nearly as much to them as what *they* say and do. Never forget that (and remember who you look for first in group photos—it's always you).

I have conducted thousands of training calls over the years. To this day, I get nervous at the beginning of each call—every single time. My ego makes me doubt myself. Am I going to sound stupid? No, I'm not. And even if I do say something wrong, I highly doubt anyone will even notice.

The greatest athletes in the world always have nerves at the beginning of every game, no matter how many years they've played the game. Nerves make us better when we fight through them. Don't let them win. Channel those nerves into excellence.

Preparation can go a very long way toward calming nerves. Subconsciously, the desire to avoid the feeling of nervousness will help you take it to the next level because it'll help you prepare. However, the flip side is that nerves can also cripple you and keep you from adequately preparing.

Don't be a cautionary tale. Recognize ego's effects and fight back by shifting into your Success Psyche. Those nerves you feel? Let them help you perform even better. Nerves can only create failure if the nervousness prevents you from moving forward. Don't let your nerves rob you of your happiness and your impact.

FIND YOUR HAPPY PLACE

If I could make someone's life better by 1 percent, that's a victory—a huge one. If my words can help one person improve their mindset by even the smallest fraction, I am living my purpose. It makes me happy just thinking about this. It also makes me happy to pursue this as a goal. That's good news for me since happiness is the center of success, and success revolves around it (not the other way around).

> Success is born out of happiness.

The happiness that we feel is what allows us to take massive action to attain success. Happiness is also what causes people to flock to you. And you need that! You need the people following you to be successful because you can't create success all by yourself. And let's be real—no one wants to follow an unhappy person.

Let's look at the word *happiness* itself for a moment. Many people don't even believe they deserve to feel happy until they reach some "destination" somewhere in the future. So, how do you strike that balance between truly being happy where you are today but still having the drive and hunger to push forward?

You don't have to be *content* with where you are. But you do have to be happy in the present moment while also determined to get where you're going. There's a difference. Being happy for the things you have and the things you've created up to this point is beautiful.

But it doesn't mean you have to stop!

One of the keys to being able to press on despite failure is to find your happy place. To get to my happy place, I spend time every morning with my daughters because my family is what makes me the most content and joyful.

No matter what's going on, how hectic life gets, you have to find that happy place.

My mom was a loving mother, but she was an unhappy person for most of her life. I remember trying to help her see the good. She had two boys who loved her. She owned a car that could get her from point A to point B. She had a roof over her head and food to eat. And that was just the tip of the iceberg.

Unfortunately, most people are programmed to focus on what they *don't* have. They fail to understand that the positive energy gained from concentrating on what they *do* have will bring even *more* of what they want into their lives.

If you are prone to focus on the negative, I challenge you to find your happy place today. Find one thing or activity that brings a smile to your face and make it a part of your daily routine.

Remember, we are programmed to fail. *Programmed* is the keyword here.

I never tell my daughters no. Don't mistake that as me saying that I let my kids get away with everything. If Luna is doing something that she shouldn't be doing, I make sure she stops doing it. But I don't just say, "No, stop." I explain the *why* behind it.

I don't want my daughters to grow up with a "no" mindset. That is damaging programming we are all subjected to as children—and it can take years to deprogram ourselves out of a negative mentality.

One key is to become aware of your negativity. To this day, I still have to catch myself because my mom and dad were both "glass-half-empty" people, and that programming can take many years to overcome. My father lived (and still lives) in a place of lack. It was never, "Yes, let's see what we can do to afford that," but rather, "No, we'll never be able to afford that."

I don't know what clicked in me. Maybe I was just tired of hearing "no" all the time. I wanted the three-stripe Adidas and the brand-name jeans, so I did what I had to do. I went into solution mode—but my father didn't teach me that.

That realization clicked in me when I was very young, but it's never too late to undo the programming from our childhood, no matter your age. Our minds essentially run on a *program* and are therefore open to re-programming.

Our brains are able to analyze new and unfamiliar situations in a way that computers can't. We can draw upon our past experiences and make inferences about new situations. We can experiment with different approaches until we find the best way to move forward. Computers cannot do that—you have to *tell* a computer what to do.

My father "lived in lack" because he existed in a state of expecting the worst-case scenario. I discovered that most people operate with a similar mindset and perpetually live in a state of survival.

The majority of the world was in survival mode during the 2020 coronavirus lockdowns. Obviously, it's essential to figure out how to stay healthy. So, survival mode has its benefits—but those benefits are few and far between.

When you're in survival mode, you're unhappy. True happiness comes when you're thriving and at the top of your game. You don't even have to be at the top of your financial pinnacle to be happy. It's not about, "I'll be happy when my bank account reaches this amount." If you think that's it, you're missing the point.

It doesn't matter what's happening around you—you can be thriving at all times. Happiness does not exist in your title or what you do for a living. It doesn't depend on a dollar amount or how the economy is doing.

> **Like motivation, happiness comes from within.**

Commit to finding that balance and being happy in who you are as a human being rather than success as a <insert job title here>.

TRANSFORMATION IS ONE PSYCHE AWAY

The world we are living in today makes it so easy to be unhappy. The "woe is me" mentality seems to be the default, and the media certainly isn't helping. During 2020, how many news stories did you see about death? Now, how many did you read about recovery? There were far more people who recovered, but we never heard those stories. That is because fear, not happiness, is what brings in advertising dollars.

"More doom and gloom; less hope" must be their unofficial motto.

Why would people want to remain fearful? You may not want to hear this, but being fearful could come from a place of laziness. It's much easier to blame other people for our problems and go on unemployment rather than search for another job and do whatever it takes to support your family. It's easy to blame our politicians for the things that happen to us. My homeless friend, who I took to McDonald's, blamed everyone else for his situation. He didn't take on an ounce of responsibility. Does that sound right to you?

Yet, it's the prevalent mentality in our country.

The COVID-19 pandemic showed me which of my friends and colleagues consciously choose to live in happiness and which ones readily allow fear to take over. Don't mistake this for me not taking COVID-19 seriously. I take it very seriously, and I do my part to protect myself and others in any way I can.

But I'm also not going to let fear ruin my life, business, or happiness.

Look, I'm no stranger to failure. In fact, I'm an expert in failure.

I've also been put here to make people realize that they have something in them that they don't even know exists. I'm in the business of empowering people and showing them how to uncover that special thing they were born to share with the world.

On paper, and given my background and upbringing, I should not be successful. Statistically speaking, I should be average at best and living paycheck to paycheck.

But I'm not. I became an outlier because I consciously chose to do a mindset shift. I purposely decided to do the hard work. And even before I fully understood that my ego was in the driver's seat, I acknowledged its control over my life.

I mean this with everything in me: *If I can make it, then anybody can make it.* I'm not special, and I'm not more intelligent than everyone else. I'm just an average guy who figured some things out and was willing to work hard and remain coachable, and now I am sharing those things with you.

We allow ourselves to be trained like dogs to behave and think a certain way. Humans domesticate animals to not pee and poop in the house, not to bite people. They're animals, but we train them to fight their instincts. We tell them not to do this and that, and when they obey, we tell our pets that they're a "good girl" or "good boy."

Humans beings are the same way. We are taught what we can and cannot do, and we blindly obey so in order to be good little girls and boys.

The *happiness advantage* (and the key to developing a Success Psyche) is not the belief that we don't need to change. *It is the realization that we can!* We can use our brains to change how we process the world, which changes how we react to it.

The most successful people, in work and in life, believe that their actions directly affect their outcomes. Constantly scanning the world for the positive allows us to experience happiness, gratitude, and optimism.

In this life, there will be many opportunities to give up. There will be times when discouragement seems to be the only emotion you feel. Other times, you'll feel like you've cracked the secret code to crushing it in life, and nothing will ever get you down. Still other days will leave you asking, *Why am I even here?*

All you can do is be the best version of yourself you can be each day. You really don't have a choice because on both the good days and the bad days, people are watching. You can't tell your kids to "look away" when you are feeling sorry for yourself or living in the past. They see it. Your team sees it. Your spouse sees it. So, do better for them and for yourself.

Take "give up" off the table altogether. When you know failure is not an option—when you don't have the safety net there anymore—you will keep looking until you find what works.

What do you want your legacy to be?

I know you want to leave a lasting one or you wouldn't have read this book in the first place. I know you and I have a lot in common, and that's how I know there is no doubt you will get tired. The next time you do, remind yourself that "tired" is a negative psyche and an excuse.

Instead of leaning into the idea of feeling "tired," become obsessed with feeding your mind positive thoughts every day. Become obsessed with being around people more successful than you. They will build you up and tell you that *everything* is possible.

You have to choose to take massive action. Otherwise, your desires will always be pipe dreams. Sadly, only a very few people ever live the life of their dreams—and that's because dream lives take massive effort and consistent action.

Your life will not change until you change your way—the way you think, the way you react, and the way you do all things.

There are so many valuable messages in books. If you are not already a voracious reader, I encourage you to become one. Like paid coaching, daily reading is an activity that has transformed my mindset and helped me see things in ways I had never seen them before.

In the first line of Chapter One, I told you that every good idea I've ever had I stole from someone else. I hope you can say the same thing after reading this book. I hope that something I have said on these pages has inspired you to go out and take your own massive action!

90-DAY
MASSIVE ACTION PLAN

Sometimes, the most challenging part of a journey is the first few steps. So, let's talk about those critical steps for a moment.

What does your success snowflake look like? Knowing that definition of success—*your unique description*—what does it mean you need to accomplish over the next ninety days? These are the kinds of questions that help you craft the mindset and routine that fosters a Success Psyche. So, if that's what you want (and why wouldn't you?), here is what needs to happen in the next ninety days:

1. **Make the daily decision.** First, you have to decide *every single day* that you will do the necessary things to transform your Success Psyche. The key phrase here is "every single day." It's not a one-time decision.

2. **Implement a morning routine.** It's time to create a morning routine that allows you to have some "me time." If this is a new habit for you, start with fifteen minutes in

each area. Don't miss this step. No matter how much time you devote to each area, your life and your Success Psyche will only reach its potential with this dedicated morning time. Get up early enough to invest in yourself at least an hour every morning. You can't be your best version unless you do this. This routine *must* include but is not limited to:

- Meditation or prayer and journaling.
- Reading at least seven to ten pages from a book daily.
- Move every day, regardless of whether it's walking, running, biking, swimming, doing yoga, lifting weights, or something else. Get your blood flowing.

3. **Become comfortable with being uncomfortable.** You must be willing to get uncomfortable daily. Remember, discomfort means growth is happening. So, don't be afraid of it. When you don't feel like doing something, DO IT!

4. **Lose the victim mentality.** Everything up to this point has happened *for* you, not to you. Lose the victim mentality. I promise you that someone else has it much worse than you, and yet they will turn tragedy into triumph. Will that be you? It's a simple decision.

5. **Don't set unrealistic expectations for others.** Remember, the only people who you can have expectations for are people you pay and yourself. Take your family and friends off the hook. It will make life much more pleasant for everyone.

6. **Define your success snowflake.** Sit down and think about what you want your life to look like. Most people never get what they want because they don't *know* what they want. What does YOUR success snowflake look like? Remember, it has to be your success, not someone else's.

7. **Recruit some accountability partners.** Share what you want and how you plan to get it with everyone in your circle. Tell everyone what your goals are, and then enroll them as accountability partners. Don't forget to give them permission to hold you accountable.

8. **Lean into failure.** You might as well start getting used to failure now. It's going to happen along the way—to everyone. There are no exceptions to this rule. So, trust the process.

9. **Define your core values.** Create your core value system and make all your decisions around them. You can use mine if they speak to you. Remember to have fun, do everything with excellence, constantly evolve your thinking, and hone your mindset.

10. **Define your why.** The final step in creating your Success Psyche is to define your why. Your why will help you do the tough things along the way that you don't feel like doing. Remember, your why can change during your journey. So revisit it each quarter and make sure it's still giving you the motivation you need to push past failure and make the daily decision to be excellent!

You can do this. I know you can. I pushed past more failures in my life than I can even remember—and what I took from each one is the lessons within them. I am stronger than I ever knew, and guess what? So are you! Maybe you aren't sure if you believe that yet. *I get it.* The process that leads to self-love, confidence, and self-acceptance can be long and painful. Just stick with it—one day at a time.

JAY ADKINS is a coach, speaker, author, and the proud owner and founder of *ProVest Insurance Group*. Jay has six insurance agencies in three regions of the United States: Florida, North Carolina, and Texas.

As co-founder and president of *Agency Sales Academy*, one of the largest sales training platforms in the country, Jay has led a bright and continuously evolving career. He's also won many awards, including Inner Circle, Chairman's, Financial Leader, Leaders-Forum, and President's Conference Awards.

He performs various consulting services for diverse industry clients, including mergers and acquisitions of insurance agencies. Jay also consults individual agency owners on effective agency operations: mindset, business optimization, effective marketing, accelerated growth, team building, and inspiration. He has also coached thousands in the network marketing space for years. In this space, he focuses on helping others develop the correct mindset, build a successful business, and be effective leaders.

Jay is passionate about training, coaching, and serving people. He's made it his life's goal to make a significant impact on the lives of every person he meets—from employees to strangers. Excellence is in every part of his life, and he feels a sense of responsibility to help others realize the excellence they want to see in theirs.

When Jay is not busy running his operation or helping others improve theirs, he can be found sailing the shimmering waters of Miami with his wife Ximena and their three children.

READY FOR MORE? GET THE PLANNER!

Success Psyche GPS is now available! It is a year-long, daily mindset mapping planner to illuminate your path to success. You will find invaluable tools to help you plan and execute your goals with precision to yield MASSIVE results! Available in bookstores and online.

Connect with me!

Let's get connected! Reach out through social media or my website and tell me how this book and planner are transforming your life.

Instagram: @jayadkins3 @thesuccessparadigm

Facebook: @jayadkins3 @thesuccessparadigm @jay.adkins.35

Podcast: //linktr.ee/thesuccessparadigm

THESUCCESSPSYCHE.COM

A free ebook edition is available with the purchase of this book.

To claim your free ebook edition:

1. Visit MorganJamesBOGO.com
2. Sign your name CLEARLY in the space
3. Complete the form and submit a photo of the entire copyright page
4. You or your friend can download the ebook to your preferred device

Morgan James
BOGO™

A **FREE** ebook edition is available for you or a friend with the purchase of this print book.

CLEARLY SIGN YOUR NAME ABOVE

Instructions to claim your free ebook edition:
1. Visit MorganJamesBOGO.com
2. Sign your name CLEARLY in the space above
3. Complete the form and submit a photo of this entire page
4. You or your friend can download the ebook to your preferred device

Print & Digital Together Forever.

Snap a photo

Free ebook

Read anywhere